COURAGE & DEFIANCE

STORIES OF SPIES, SABOTEURS, AND SURVIVORS IN WORLD WAR II DENMARK

BY DEBORAH HOPKINSON

SCHOLASTIC
FOCUS

NEW YORK

Copyright © 2015 by Deborah Hopkinson

This book was originally published in hardcover by Scholastic Press in 2015.

All rights reserved. Published by Scholastic Focus, a division of Scholastic Inc., *Publishers since 1920.* SCHOLASTIC, SCHOLASTIC FOCUS, and associated logos are trademarks and/or registered trademarks of Scholastic Inc.

The publisher does not have any control over and does not assume any responsibility for author or third-party websites or their content.

No part of this publication may be reproduced, stored in a retrieval system, or transmitted in any form or by any means, electronic, mechanical, photocopying, recording, or otherwise, without written permission of the publisher. For information regarding permission, write to Scholastic Inc., Attention: Permissions Department, 557 Broadway, New York, NY 10012.

ISBN 978-0-545-59221-5

10 9 8 7 6 5 4 3   20

Printed in the U.S.A.   40
First printing 2016

Book design by Phil Falco

For Lisa Sandell

This is an extraordinary time we're living in, and it has brought forth many extraordinary people. . . . Never has the world been exposed to such suffering, but never has the feeling of life been as strong or as intense as now.

—Kim Malthe-Bruun, November 28, 1944

• CONTENTS •

German soldiers during the invasion of Denmark.

• PROLOGUE •

Imagine waking up one morning to find foreign soldiers standing on the street corners of your town. Overnight, an enemy army has arrived and now occupies your entire country. This is what happened on April 9, 1940, when Germany invaded Denmark in World War II.

Imagine being pulled out of school one morning and told that you and your family are in mortal danger and must go into hiding and leave the country immediately. This is what happened on September 29, 1943, when warnings spread through the Jewish community in Denmark that they were about to be captured and deported to a concentration camp.

Courage & Defiance tells the stories of real people who experienced these events. This book doesn't capture everything that happened in Denmark during World War II, or attempt to cover the entire history of the war. I hope to help illuminate this time through the stories of a few people who were faced with life-changing decisions when war arrived on their doorsteps.

Courage & Defiance is an introduction to a multifaceted, complex story, and there are many aspects I have not addressed. These include in-depth explorations of the political situation, the underground press, and collaborators and Nazi sympathizers. I have only touched on the important role that the Danish Communist Party and its affiliated sabotage group, BOPA, played throughout the occupation, especially in helping to build an organized movement and inciting resistance and sabotage. I hope readers whose curiosity is sparked by this time period will seek out other books and resources, and I have included suggestions in the Bibliography and Other Resources section.

The German occupation of Denmark lasted five years, from April 1940 until May 1945. This book is organized in a chronological manner, but you'll find that the threads of stories within it sometimes intertwine, intersect, disappear, and then reappear. After all, the past, like our own present, is a messy business—a crazy quilt rather than a straight line of names and events to be memorized.

Denmark's experiences during World War II are unique. The country was never officially at war with Germany. Danish resistance efforts came about not from government policies or programs, but from the actions of individuals who risked their lives to challenge the occupying force and their own government's policy of adapting to Germany's power.

But World War II was not just a military conflict. The Nazis carried out the worst atrocities in human history in the Holocaust, which saw the murder of six million Jewish men, women, and children from more than twenty countries, including Germany, the Soviet Union, Poland, Austria, Hungary, Romania, France, and the Netherlands. Believing that Germans were a superior race and that Jews represented a threat, the Nazis implemented a horrific plan, which they called the Final Solution, to systematically imprison innocent people in concentration camps, where they were tortured, starved, and murdered.

This did not happen in Denmark. Approximately 7,700 Jews lived in Denmark before the war; 7,220 were rescued, fewer than 475 were captured, and 53 died in concentration camps. Historians estimate that perhaps another 20 to 60 people died attempting to escape, for a total of 75 to 120 victims. In other words, unlike in many other countries, most of the Danish Jews survived, thanks to a spontaneous, grassroots rescue effort undertaken by ordinary people: college students, teachers, professors, mechanics, fishermen, police officers. Nor were those taken away forgotten by their fellow citizens: The Danes worked to send food and clothing to prisoners and negotiated their early release.

Noted historian Lani Yahil, who compiled a detailed account of the rescue efforts, writes that the Danish story has much to teach us, especially about how people and nations can remain true to their humanity and to their values, even under tremendous pressure. "This remarkable rescue stands out as a praiseworthy and heroic event—and that is how it ought to be remembered for all time."

I was struck by something else Dr. Yahil said, which is reflected in the memoirs and stories I read of those who participated in the Danish resistance. Dr. Yahil notes that people who took part in the rescue didn't think of themselves as heroes, rather "they merely did the natural and necessary, and never for a moment considered the possibility of abandoning the Jews to their fate.

"It was clear to each and every one that this was the thing to do."

. . .

Danish is to many of us an unfamiliar language, so some of the names may be confusing. To help readers keep track, I've used first names for those people whose lives we follow most closely, as well as a few others. Historical figures and others are usually identified by last name. I have also included a list of the major people mentioned in this book, at the end. Also, if you want to hear Danish, check out the About Danish section, which includes a description of the Danish alphabet and a link to hear it spoken online.

Also included in the back matter are a map of Denmark and a list of other books for further reading. While I've indicated books that may be of special interest to young readers, many of the other resources mentioned make for fascinating reading. Dr. Nathaniel Hong, who kindly read and commented on the manuscript of this book, has written two books on the Danish resistance. He first became curious about it while living in Copenhagen at the age of twelve.

But a book can only go so far to make history come alive. You can also hear and see oral histories of Holocaust survivors and Jews who escaped Denmark (including Herbert Pundik, who appears in these pages) by visiting the website of the United States Holocaust Memorial Museum and by looking online at photos at the Museum of Danish Resistance.

I first became aware of the Danish resistance through Lois Lowry's Newbery-winning book *Number the Stars*, a fictional account of this time and the rescue of the Jews, a novel that my children and I all loved. After completing my book, I went back again to read *Number the Stars* and in the afterword recognized the name of Kim Malthe-Bruun, who inspired Lois Lowry. Quite separately, his words had touched me as I was researching, and you'll find excerpts of his letters in these pages.

In October 2014, a few weeks before his ninety-fifth birthday, I had the honor to meet Niels Skov, whose story is told in this book, and his wife, Diane, at their home in Washington State. Although he was gravely ill, Niels's indomitable, resolute spirit shone through, just as it must have done seventy-four years ago when he found the courage to defy the oppressors who had invaded his homeland. I hope his story, and those of other brave men and women who fought for freedom, justice, and equality, will inspire you as they have me.

German troops on a street in Copenhagen after the invasion of Denmark.

PART ONE

OCCUPATION &
THE SPARKS OF DEFIANCE
APRIL 1940–AUGUST 1943

I feel that I must always follow my inner convictions, always be prepared for the unexpected, always be ready to spring into action . . . living for the moment only and with our lives at stake. The group with which I'm working has completely accepted this.

—Kim Malthe-Bruun, November 28, 1944

occupation (n): the action, state, or period of occupying or being occupied by military force.

sabotage (v): to deliberately destroy, damage, or obstruct (something), especially for political or military advantage.

spy (v): to work for a government or other organization by secretly obtaining information about enemies or competitors.

APRIL 9, 1940: INVASION

Copenhagen, Denmark, Tuesday, April 9. German troops crossed the Danish frontier at 5 o'clock this morning. . . . The invasion came without warning.

—*The New York Times*, April 9, 1940

It happened overnight.

In the early morning hours of an early spring day, a twenty-year-old apprentice toolmaker named Niels Skov was cleaning his workbench at the end of his night shift when some day workers began to file in. Niels noticed them clustering together, murmuring in low, uneasy voices. He wondered what was wrong.

As he went to the clock to stamp his time card, a fellow apprentice gave him some startling news. "'Niels, there are foreign soldiers in town.'"

Niels hurried out and hopped on his bicycle to see for himself. At first everything looked normal: The people of Copenhagen were heading to work or school. Just as Niels did, most people commuted by bicycle.

Then, in front of the British embassy, Niels saw something unusual: two soldiers in uniforms. Looking closer, he saw they weren't wearing the light gray of the Danish army. Instead, they were dressed in a darker, unfamiliar gray green. "I slowed and rode by them looking as unconcerned as possible. They were about my age, nervously scanning the quiet street in

German troops on the march in Copenhagen, April 1940.

both directions, and close up I saw the German insignia on their helmets."

Niels pedaled home, hoping to find out more on the radio. When he burst into the apartment, his mother confirmed what he'd seen: " 'They say the Germans are rolling into Jutland.' "

It was almost impossible to believe. Everything had happened so quickly. The day before had been ordinary. Niels and his fellow citizens had gone to work or school. People shopped for groceries, took care of little ones. In the evening, families ate dinner together before turning in for the night—like any other night. That was Monday.

Then came Tuesday, April 9, 1940. Suddenly the sky buzzed with menacing foreign airplanes, hundreds of them. People bicycling to or from work encountered German soldiers in the streets—their own, familiar, well-loved streets. Overnight, the

A column of German forces moves past villagers of a small Danish town on April 9, 1940.

small nation of Denmark had been overtaken by Germany, its large and powerful neighbor to the south.

World War II had come to Denmark.

...

Why was this happening? To understand some of the causes for Germany's aggression and World War II itself, we can look as far back as 1919, when the Treaty of Versailles was signed at the end of World War I. That treaty forced Germany to accept responsibility for causing the war and demanded heavy reparations. Many Germans felt resentful about the conditions it imposed.

In the years to follow, as Germany became the dominant power in Europe, the flames of resentment and nationalism were fueled by one man, who rose to power as a popular leader and stood against the Weimar Republic, the democratic German government that had been put in place in 1919. His name was Adolf Hitler.

When Hitler became the German chancellor in 1933, he began transforming Germany from a parliamentary democracy into a totalitarian dictatorship called the Third Reich, based on the principles of the Nazi Party (Nationalsozialistische Deutsche Arbeiterpartei in German, or NSDAP, the National Socialist German Workers' Party. *Nazi* comes from the word Nationalsozialist.) Nazism was a right-wing, racist, nationalist movement, which held that the so-called Aryan race was supreme. Hitler, who could sway large crowds with his fiery speeches, became the country's sole leader, or führer.

Under Hitler, Germany began making aggressive grabs for neighboring countries, including Austria and Czechoslovakia. At first, attempting to avoid military conflict, Great Britain and

Adolf Hitler.

France tried to go along, following a policy called appeasement. Then, on September 1, 1939, Germany invaded Poland. Two days later, because of their alliances with Poland, Great Britain and France declared war on Germany.

Appeasement had come to an end. World War II had begun.

• • •

On that fateful morning of April 9, 1940, Niels and his mother stayed glued to the radio. By midmorning, the Danish king, King Christian X, had come on the air to advise his citizens to remain calm and go about their normal lives. Normal? Nothing seemed normal to Niels anymore. Nothing *was* normal.

Niels headed back outside to find out what his fellow Danes were making of these incredible events. "Riding along,

King Christian X on his horse.

CHAPTER ONE

I kept scanning people's faces. My countrymen appeared to go about their business as usual. A bit concerned, worried perhaps, but obviously with no inclination to fight."

Niels felt surprised that no one appeared as upset as he himself felt. Just looking at those invaders made him "enraged, embarrassed, ashamed."

Niels was angry, brash, and confident. He wasn't about to be intimidated—not even by a terrifying show of force and power on his very doorstep. He sized up the soldiers. "So this was what Hitler's troops looked like close up: my own age, and clearly apprehensive about being on enemy, or at least foreign territory. Silently, I measured myself against them and thought that I would be willing and able to take on any one of them."

A German tank rolls through Denmark on the day of the invasion.

At that moment he made up his mind. "I saw with complete certainty that I was going to fight, somewhere, somehow. There was hardly a decision process involved; it was simply so."

Niels knew nothing about resistance or sabotage or war. He certainly didn't have any sort of plan. But he had taken the first step: the decision to act.

■ ■ ■

Niels Skov wasn't the only one outraged by the overnight invasion. Twenty-year-old Jørgen Kieler was a struggling medical student who shared an apartment in Copenhagen with his brother, Flemming, and two sisters, Elsebet and Bente. The Kieler siblings were dedicated to getting a college education. Often that meant saving money however they could: cooking lots of stews and carrots at home instead of eating out, and even riding their bicycles to see their parents in their hometown of Horsens for the holidays (a chilly 155 miles in December!).

"We heated the flat using stoves, when there was fuel to be had," recalled Jørgen. Their apartment didn't have hot water. "There was cold running water, but if we wanted to have a bath, we had to go to the Copenhagen Public Baths."

Winters were the worst. "We froze," recalled Jørgen. "Sometimes there was even ice on our bedsheets when we woke up in the morning. We could hardly ever get hold of coal." To stay warm they studied in the university library.

On that April morning, when Jørgen and Elsebet first heard the menacing rumble of airplanes, they had no idea if the planes were British, Danish, or German. It didn't take long to find out.

"We got dressed hurriedly and walked out onto the street," Jørgen said. "At the corner . . . I saw my first German soldier, who was standing right in the middle of the thoroughfare with fixed bayonet and hand grenades hanging from his belt. He was surrounded by a group of inquisitive cyclists."

The Germans had appeared so quickly Jørgen guessed (correctly) that there'd been no significant counterattack by the Danish military: The Danish government must have given up overnight. "We felt boundless shame and sadness when we realized that Denmark had, in effect, capitulated without resistance, despite the assurances of politicians that they were going to defend us."

German bombers fly over Copenhagen on April 9, 1940, dropping leaflets to the streets below.

In the weeks and months that followed, Jørgen got used to blackouts, food rationing, and even to seeing German soldiers on the streets day in and day out. But he couldn't shake the frustration of being under German occupation. He felt powerless to do anything about it—except go on with his studies. "In 1940, my brother, sisters and I had no way of escaping our feeling of paralysis other than by immersing ourselves in our work."

Jørgen realized he was lucky to be able to go to school and still lead a relatively normal life. Denmark was not officially at war with Germany, so he wasn't required to become a soldier. He could continue to prepare for his future as a doctor.

Jørgen didn't feel ready to become a resistance fighter yet. But the question of how he should protest Denmark's occupation was never far from his mind. Jørgen and his friends debated what they could do to resist the Germans and how they could help their small country in the face of the powerful enemy now present on their streets.

It would take Jørgen many months—years even—before he found a path to resistance. When he did, it would demand more than he could ever imagine of himself and his family.

• • •

Thomas Sneum was as idealistic as Niels Skov and Jørgen Kieler—and just as angry at the sudden invasion. When the first German planes filled the skies, Tommy (as he was nicknamed), a young flight lieutenant in Denmark's small air force, wanted nothing more than to be up in the air battling for his country. The order to fly never came.

The truth was that the entire Danish military was completely outmatched by the Germans. With only nine thousand army troops, fewer than five thousand naval officers and men, and a small air force at their command, Danish officials knew it would be suicidal to mount a military response to the invasion. Only one Danish aircraft tried to take off on April 9. It was shot down, while another twenty-five planes were damaged by German fire as they sat motionless on the ground.

There were other reasons not to resist. A small, mostly flat country, Denmark has no natural defenses, such as high mountains. Unlike Norway, where an approaching army might be slowed down by dynamiting or blockading a mountain road, in Denmark there is not much that can be done to stop invaders, who can just "drive or march through the adjoining flat field."

Denmark is also an island country. The largest landmass is Jutland, a peninsula that connects on the south to Germany and lies between the North Sea (to the west) and the Baltic Sea. The rest of the nation is composed of about five hundred islands, with people living on one hundred or so of them. The capital city of Copenhagen is situated on the island of Zealand, which at its narrowest point is only three miles across the Øresund Sound (often just called the Sound) from Sweden to the west.

During World War I (1914–1918), Denmark, like its Scandinavian neighbors Norway and Sweden, had managed to remain neutral. All these countries hoped to stay out of the new conflict too. Yet as the war in Europe escalated, this began to seem unlikely. In early 1940, before becoming prime minister later that year, Great Britain's Winston Churchill put it bluntly: "'I have not the slightest doubt that the Germans will swarm over Denmark when it suits them.'"

Denmark, which lies between Germany and Norway, was simply "a convenient stepping stone." The real prize was Norway. Norway was critical because its port of Narvik offered a harbor free of winter ice, which meant an uninterrupted supply of iron ore and other resources needed for the war effort. Rumors had been circulating that both Germany and Great Britain were eyeing Norway. By the winter of 1940, the real question was which country would make the first move. Hitler beat the British to it, launching an invasion of Norway and Denmark on that same April day.

The operation to occupy Denmark unfolded like clockwork. Unbeknownst to the Danes, in the early days of April the noose was already tightening: The Germans were moving armored cars, tanks, trucks, motorcycles, and even bicycles, as well as two regiments of infantry soldiers on foot, closer to the Danish border.

On April 7, 1940, disguised as a civil servant, a German major general named Kurt Himer flew into Copenhagen. (His military uniform was stashed in a companion's suitcase.) While in Denmark, Himer met with the German ambassador, delivering sealed instructions that were to be conveyed to the Danish government once the invasion began.

Himer also scouted the harbor area to make sure that the ship that would be carrying a battalion of German troops could dock easily. Himer reported everything he learned back to Germany by telephone and made arrangements to set up a radio communications headquarters in Copenhagen. He wanted to be in contact with German officials as the invasion unfolded, especially if the Danes cut phone lines.

At 4:00 a.m. on Tuesday, April 9, 1940, the German ambassador requested an emergency meeting with Denmark's foreign minister to give him the news. The German government had "'set in motion certain military operations which will lead to the occupation of strategic points on Danish soil.'" Further, the ambassador warned, any attempts at resistance by the Danish government would have serious consequences. King Christian X, who was nearly seventy, was awakened and briefed on the grave danger facing his nation.

The invasion launched at 4:15 a.m. German troops were deployed to ports, airfields, harbors, and the country's military bases, taking Danish military leaders by surprise. The Germans were thorough: They secured airfields, along with key bridges, ferry terminals, ports, and roads. German planes dropped leaflets warning the citizens of Denmark that if they resisted, Copenhagen and other Danish cities would be bombed.

"I will never forget it," said Leo Goldberger, who was nine at the time. "It is still as vivid in my memory as if it were yesterday. . . . The early morning sky was blackened by low-flying planes. From my window I reached out to catch a green leaflet coming down from the sky like confetti."

At the palace in Copenhagen, scattered shots broke the dawn silence. The king's first order to his guards had been to resist. Yet it soon became apparent that the Germans were

German planes fly over a Danish village during the invasion of Denmark in April 1940.

already in control. King Christian didn't have a chance of escape, where he might rule in exile. Recognizing that it was too late, orders were given to halt resistance to the invaders.

It was all over by 7:20 a.m.

■ ■ ■

For the Danish people, the future was uncertain. For all anyone knew, April 9, 1940, might be the start of a new, long chapter in their history. If the Germans won the war—and in those early months Germany seemed unbeatable—Denmark would most likely become part of a large Nazi empire.

That's why Jørgen Kieler felt that everything he loved about his country, even Danish culture and language, was at stake. That's why Niels Skov made a personal vow to act, and Tommy Sneum soon asked for a discharge and left military service to create a resistance plan of his own.

From this day on, these three young people and others like them began to search for ways to defy the Germans occupying their land. The Danish resistance effort didn't burst into full action overnight. Rather it grew over a period of months and years, with starts and stops, heartbreaking setbacks, and small victories. It was sometimes scattered and unorganized, with well-meaning and inexperienced people trying to work together under extremely difficult conditions. It took immense courage, and it cost lives.

But it began that first day, when ordinary citizens woke up to a changed world. It began with anger, disbelief, and determination. And it began with individuals asking themselves a difficult, almost impossible question: What can one person—or even a few together—do to make a difference against a powerful invading force?

As it happens, it wasn't too long before Niels Skov came up with an answer.

A SINGLE MATCH

Things had changed in Copenhagen. Niels Skov could feel it. His city had sometimes been called the Paris of the North, a place that came alive at night, with bright lights and friends gathering together for lively conversation. Since the invasion, though, Copenhagen was like a living being that had been struck down. The whole city "lay inert and invisible, as if stunned by events beyond comprehension."

Niels could sense changes within himself too. Pedaling his bicycle alone along dark, silent streets, he realized that living under German occupation had touched a chord deep inside him, a sort of "primal, defensive instinct" that wouldn't go away.

He was especially frustrated with his own government. Danish officials had urged citizens to adopt a "'quiet and restrained demeanor in the conditions now prevailing.'" In other words, don't rock the boat, because that would just make things worse. That didn't sit well with the impatient Niels. His response was simple: "Well, they could shove that piece of advice."

Yet what actions *could* Niels take on his own? His bicycle rides provided the answer. As he traveled around the city, Niels noticed German military vehicles parked on the streets overnight. That gave him an idea: Why not burn a car?

Niels didn't have explosives, nor did he have a clue where to get anything like that. Maybe, though, all he needed was one match. And so several months into the occupation, on a fall night after he'd left his job and started engineering school, Niels began what he called his "private war against the Germans."

This kind of stealthy sabotage seemed a good way to begin. It wouldn't harm anyone physically, but it would certainly annoy the Germans. At least he would be taking a stand. He would be doing *something*. All in all, Niels decided, it was "attractive and probably easy, a satisfactory way of doing noticeable damage."

As he roamed the city on his evening bike rides, Niels took to carrying matches as well as a treasured homemade screwdriver his grandfather had given him. Then, on a still October night, it happened. "It was ten o'clock, and the street lay dark and quiet. The German staff car was parked at the curb in the middle of the block, its camouflage paint rendering it all but invisible until I was almost near enough to touch it."

Dismounting and checking that the coast was clear, Niels scrambled down to the pavement and slid under the car. "With my left hand I placed the sharp point of the screwdriver against the bottom of the fuel tank and struck the tool a silent blow with my right, piercing the tank just slightly and starting a drip-drop of gasoline onto the pavement.

"Sliding free of the car, I got up and checked again that the street was silent. Satisfied, I got the book of matches out . . . struck one and threw it under the car where the gasoline drip had already made a small wet spot."

As Niels watched, "The fuel caught with a bright yellow flame, larger than I had expected, and it momentarily illuminated the little street scene with me in the center. I grabbed my bike, jumped on and sped off."

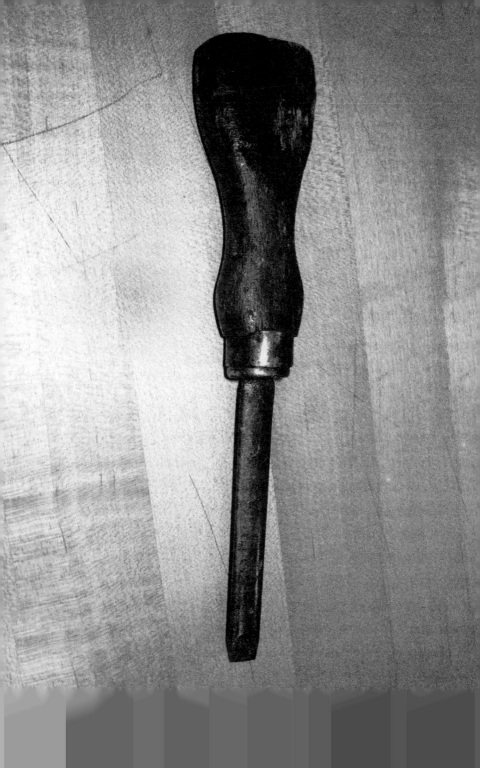

German airplanes land on Værløse Airfield in Denmark on April 9, 1940.

At the end of the street he stopped to look. "The fire had grown rapidly, and about one minute after I had struck the match, the gas tank exploded, illuminating the street and buildings on both sides. The street was still empty."

Niels forced himself not to hurry. Safe in bed an hour later, he thought about what he'd done. It had been remarkably easy, yet he knew it was dangerous. "I also realized how far out of step I was with the rest of the population."

Niels was right. Lighting that one match meant he'd crossed a line from peaceful citizen to saboteur. Sabotage was against the law. Niels could be arrested not only by the Germans, but also by the Danish police. While individual officers might be sympathetic to the cause of resistance, the police force itself was caught in the middle. Danish police

CHAPTER TWO

were charged with trying to keep unrest from bubbling up into open resistance, which would result in Germany exerting harsher measures of control over Denmark and her people.

Although Niels was well aware that what he'd done was both dangerous and illegal, in the end he decided that didn't matter. It had been his first planned, successful act. It wouldn't be his last. "Just wait . . ." he silently addressed the enemy. "There are more matches where these came from."

•••

In a way, we can say that the Danish resistance began with individuals like Niels Skov holding a single match. Yet it would take a long time for the smoldering embers of defiance to burst into flames. While Niels had begun to follow a path of opposition that would change his life, most people continued with their regular day-to-day activities.

Schools were still open; businesses continued to operate; the streets were peaceful. Danish farms were feeding not only the local population, but Germany as well. And, unlike what was happening in Germany and other countries it had invaded, Jewish families in Denmark were not being harassed, arrested, or deported to concentration camps.

Still, below the surface, tensions simmered. Denmark was not officially at war with Germany, but the Nazis had control over Danish military bases and its transportation systems, although Denmark had been allowed to keep a small army of about five thousand. Germany had promised not to interfere in Denmark's internal affairs but put pressure on Danish officials to meet its demands. This included ensuring that Danish factories sent supplies and goods to Germany, as well as keeping the Danish populace under control.

For instance, resistance to the German occupation was against the law, and the German authorities expected the cooperation of the Danish police to crack down on anyone who stepped out of line. Ordinary citizens were on their own: During the war years, there was never a free Danish government that could authorize resistance. In fact, the more the Danish people acted against the Nazis, the more pressure Germany put on the Danish government and police to restrain them.

One historian explained it this way: "The Danish Resistance had to be created without the slightest scrap of authority, and the first resistants had to face not only a difficult situation but a most serious responsibility. They entered the field knowing that if they succeeded, their fellow-countrymen would have to take the consequences."

Nevertheless, grassroots resistance bubbled up almost immediately. An early protest method was distributing leaflets. One that circulated in the fall of 1940 was called *Song of Denmark*. It included these stanzas:

Lovely Denmark with forested coasts
If only we were free of every last German
Gone is security. Gone is tranquility
Peace has vanished where the German lives.

Lovely Denmark with cows and pigs
Everything you own the Germans can take

Now they will reap what we must sow
And put a muzzle on us in return.

The *Song of Denmark* was copied by hand or typed out, and passed from one person to another at workplaces, schools, and among friends and relatives. The Danish police worked hard to trace the source of the leaflets. About twenty-five people were charged and sentenced to a week or several weeks in jail for distributing the song, but many more participated. Other leaflets urged passive resistance, advising people to avoid talking to German soldiers and to give them the cold shoulder.

Other early resistance tactics included posters, student demonstrations, and graffiti with slogans such as "Down with Hitler." Stickers with anti-German messages calling for Denmark's freedom were pasted on mailboxes, on lampposts, and near tram stops.

At movie theaters, German newsreels were shown before the feature film. To vent their disapproval, audiences would shout out anti-Hitler slogans or stamp their feet. Local police advised theater owners to turn on the lights and tell people the film would be shown only if this kind of disruptive behavior stopped. To reinforce that message, theaters showed a slide reminding people that King Christian had called on everyone to have "correct behavior."

Individual police officers were often sympathetic. Knud Dyby, who actively supported the resistance, recalled being sent to a theater where young people were trying to disrupt the showing of a German film. "'I did not want to arrest the young people, who were obviously resisting in their own way, but I was a policeman and I had to do something. I took the movie reel, handed one end of the film to a member of the group and ordered them all to leave. When they ran away, I put my shoe lightly on the film as it dragged along the floor, scratching it thoroughly so it could not be shown again. I reported back to my superiors that a gang had destroyed the film.' "

Another protest action that came under scrutiny was spitting on the street in the direction of German soldiers. It happened so often that a Copenhagen police officer tried to explain it away by saying that Danes chewed more tobacco than Germans.

It's no surprise that people tried to voice their anger and frustration in these ways. Stamping one's feet in protest in a dark movie theater could be a first step to further commitment—but far less risky than setting fire to a car. Historian Nathaniel Hong notes that "dissidents to official policy were forced to first find their voice through the communication strategies of the powerless: graffiti, leaflets, stickers, pins, and the occasional shout of defiance in the movie theatre."

Together, these efforts helped to break down the isolation and frustration Danish people felt. Besides, almost anyone could do something as simple as passing around a leaflet.

Tommy Sneum, on the other hand, had something entirely different in mind.

STALKING A SECRET INSTALLATION

One night, late in the summer of 1940, Tommy Sneum left his bed and slipped outside. He was on Fanø, the small island off the southwest coast of Denmark in the North Sea where he'd grown up. Curious to get a better look at the German defense installation nearby, he crept over the island's sandy dunes and made his way through its small, stunted pines.

Suddenly he heard the drone of a plane. As the sound grew louder, Tommy could see the outline of a strange, rectangular piece of machinery on the other side of the installation fence. The mysterious machine began to swivel, then a searchlight switched on. That's when Tommy spotted a silver plane overhead. The beam hit the plane precisely.

A Spitfire I, flown by the British RAF.

Tommy could guess what it meant. He'd made a point to become friendly with some German officers, sometimes having beers with them at a local restaurant. These attempts to act as an undercover agent didn't go over well with his old friends, who suspected him of being pro-German.

But Tommy's efforts had paid off—big-time. One night, when he'd casually asked an officer if the Germans were afraid of the British bombing the Fanø installation, the man had let something slip. "'They'd never reach us. . . . We'd be able to see them coming from far away. . . . We've got special technology.'"

Special technology. What might that be? Tommy was determined to find out. Now he was seeing it in action for the first time, and it "'made me certain we were dealing with some kind of early-warning system. I was convinced that they now had the capability to plot the position of a ship or plane using radio waves.'"

Tommy was sure of something else too: If the Germans had a new early-warning system in place, it could spell disaster for British pilots. While he had no way of knowing whether Great Britain was aware of Germany's new invention, which he learned later was called Freya radar, he wasn't about to leave anything to chance. Here was something meaningful he could do on his own: Warn the British. It might also be a way to get into the war as a pilot. If he could escape Denmark and get to Great Britain, he might be allowed to join the British Royal Air Force.

Tommy wanted to be the one to deliver the information. He decided to try to get to the neutral country of Sweden, where the British had an embassy. He would then tell the British what

Tommy Sneum.

he'd learned and offer himself up as a volunteer pilot. So in February 1941, posing as a Danish businessman, Tommy made it to the British legation in Stockholm, where he met with Captain Henry Denham, a naval attaché. Denham listened to Tommy's report, although he didn't seem as impressed as Tommy had hoped. Instead, he wanted Tommy to return to Denmark to get more evidence, saying, " 'We need to understand exactly how these things work. Get as much technical detail as we can.'

" 'I don't see what more I could do,' replied Sneum.

" 'You could take photographs,' suggested Denham."

Photographs? Tommy was skeptical. He couldn't imagine just strolling up to the restricted military installation like a tourist with a camera slung over his shoulder.

" 'You could use a little Leica,' continued Denham calmly. 'Nothing too conspicuous. And if that works out, you could use a Movikon camera. They take moving pictures.' "

Tommy agreed to try. In March 1941, equipped with two cameras, untrained and untested, he became an unofficial spy for Great Britain. His mission: Get pictures and details on the new Freya radar machinery at a top secret installation.

Tommy's first break came when he boarded the ferry from the town of Esbjerg over to Fanø. As the ferry was about to set off, Tommy noticed that the engine had paused so that a last piece of equipment could be lowered by a crane onto the deck. Instantly alert, Tommy casually positioned himself for a closer look at what appeared to be some sort of control cabin. Could it have something to do with the German military installation on Fanø?

CHAPTER THREE

Tommy shot a quick glance around. No one was paying attention to him. "'I couldn't believe it. This was too good to be true, and I wasn't about to miss my chance.'"

The door of the cabin had swung open as it was being lowered to the deck. Standing as close as he dared, Tommy grabbed his camera and snapped a few pictures from different angles. "'It was one of the most dangerous moments but also one of the most satisfying.'"

Once on Fanø, Tommy began making plans to get shots of the Freya equipment. Realizing that he'd need to get as close as possible to the installation in daylight, he decided to pose as a hunter. Along with his camera, Tommy took a gun and even bagged some rabbits on the heath to make his story believable if he was stopped. Then he began to scout the installation, watching the guards closely as they patrolled the fences.

He needed to choose his moment carefully. Tommy knew that if he was caught, he'd likely be arrested, tortured, and maybe even executed by the Nazis. Once he had the guards' routine timing down, he figured he had about one minute of safety when he could stand out in the open to snap pictures. He took as many pictures of the towers as he dared, then darted back under cover.

Tommy also wanted to show the radar in action. That meant using the primitive movie camera the Movikon, which was larger than the tiny Leica and would be a lot harder to carry inconspicuously. He would take the risk. Tommy asked a local friend named Peter, whom he knew was sympathetic to the cause, to help out. This time they would take bicycles. Peter would stand guard while Tommy shot the footage.

Tommy planned to wait until a plane came into view so he could capture the warning system in action. As the two rode their bicycles close to the trees near the installation, Tommy noticed that the sensors had started to rotate as the radar located an aircraft. Quickly he pulled out the camera from under his jacket and began filming.

Nearby, Peter hissed a frantic warning. " 'There's somebody coming.' " Peter sped off on his bike, while Tommy tucked the camera under his jacket.

Tommy thought fast. He somehow had to create a diversion—a believable diversion—and he had to do it right then and there. The solution he came up with might seem comical, but it was all he could think of at the moment.

" 'I crouched down in the tall grass. In that squatting position, my knees were sticking out. That helped to hide the bulge created by the movie camera under my jacket. At the same time I pulled down my trousers and pants. The German officer came up with his rifle pointed at me. This was one of the most dangerous moments of my entire war. If he made me get up he would see the bulge of the camera and soon know I was a spy.' "

The soldier asked what he was doing, and Tommy replied crudely in German, pretending to be annoyed at his privacy being disturbed! The ploy worked. To Tommy's relief, the man was so embarrassed he walked off without asking any more questions. As soon as he'd gone, Tommy jumped up, pulled up his pants, hopped on his bicycle, and was off. Tommy had been lucky—he knew he wouldn't have been able to pull off this trick with a more experienced guard.

CHAPTER THREE

Although Tommy had escaped, the shots he'd managed to take were too far away to show details of the new radar technology. He'd have to try again.

...

Three days later Tommy made his next move. This time he would go alone. After scouting the area further he'd come up with a new plan. He would station himself at the foot of a water tower close to the installation. Trees grew close to it on one side. If he used those as cover he was fairly sure he could get to the right spot without being seen. There would be guards posted right over him, he knew, but that was simply a risk he'd have to take.

" 'Their blind spot was at the foot of the water tower itself. . . . When you are up in the tower, you are not going to be looking directly below you for the enemy, in your own area. You are going to be looking out to sea for ships or aircraft.' "

Tommy set out under the cover of darkness up the wooded hill to the water tower. Once there, he was so close he could hear the voices of the guards above, chatting in German. Tommy waited for dawn, then for something to happen. At last a plane approached.

Tommy clicked on his camera, capturing the large, revolving structure as it followed the path of the aircraft. This time if he got caught, there would be no fooling the Nazis. When he noticed the guards above moving to look in a different direction, he decided that was enough. Slipping the camera under his jacket, he bolted back under the cover of trees and took off.

Part of him waited for the order to halt. "'I had already decided to keep running if that happened, even if it meant I risked being shot in the back. . . . To be captured would have meant torture.'" As he made his way through the woods, all he could hear was the sound of his own breath. "'I wanted to shout with joy, but I couldn't.'"

Tommy Sneum had done it: He had captured Freya radar in action. What he had found might help save lives, not just in Denmark but also in other parts of Europe. If the Germans were using this equipment here, it might well be part of their defense systems elsewhere. While it might be possible to sneak into Sweden, Tommy thought the danger of carrying the bulky film reels was too high. He'd risked his life for these shots; he needed to get his precious reels into the right hands.

Tommy made up his mind. He would deliver the films to London himself. And so he began planning one of the most daring feats of World War II.

HELP FROM AFAR: THE SOE, CHURCHILL'S SECRET ARMY

In the fall of 1940, while Niels Skov was launching a sabotage campaign and Tommy Sneum was stalking a German military installation, another man, far from Denmark, was about to become part of its wartime story.

Born in England on November 20, 1912, Ralph Hollingworth had left home to travel when he was eighteen. He'd ended up in Copenhagen, where he learned Danish and worked in a bicycle shop. While there, it also seems likely he dabbled in intelligence work for Britain's Royal Navy.

Fast-forward to October 1940. In Iceland as an officer in the naval reserves, Ralph received an order to return to Great Britain. A veil of secrecy shrouded his new assignment. "'I was to go to London and report at a given address, bring two sets of old clothes,'" Ralph recalled. From there, he and another man, Ronald Turnbull, were sent to a house in the countryside.

"'Here we were told to ring the bell, and the door was opened by an oldish servant, who asked for our names. When we gave them, he stopped us and whispered two other names, which we understood we were to use in the future instead of our own.'"

It wasn't until Ralph had received some basic training in covert operations that he learned the exact nature of his new top secret assignment. He'd been tapped to head the Danish

Ralph Hollingworth.

section of a new organization called the Special Operations Executive (SOE). Ralph would be based in London, while Turnbull would be posted to Stockholm. Their mission: "'to raise a Resistance struggle in Denmark, and organize it.'"

"'I had to start absolutely from scratch,'" Ralph later wrote. "'How it was to be done, it was up to me to find out. I got a little office (in Baker Street) with the barest office necessities, telephone, correspondence trays, etc.—and had to find out how to set about it.'"

• • •

The SOE was formed in July 1940, during some of the bleakest months of the war. It was a dark time for Great Britain, which was struggling alone to face what one historian has called "an apparently unstoppable" Nazi Germany. That's where the SOE came in. It was set up to expand traditional military actions by helping to organize and support resistance efforts from *inside* enemy-occupied territories. The SOE would use unconventional means, disrupting German authority, power, and war operations in countries under German occupation.

Historian Knud Jespersen described the SOE's goals this way: The SOE would "foster the spirit of resistance and encourage a resistance movement that, through acts of sabotage, would wear down and weaken the Germans as much as possible and thereby, make some contribution to Britain's struggle for survival." In short, the SOE was to be a secret sabotage and spy operation. Few people knew of its existence; for this reason, it's sometimes been called Churchill's Secret Army.

Ronald Turnbull.

The SOE was organized into different sections by countries: France, Norway, Denmark, Belgium, the Netherlands, Poland, Italy, and Germany itself, to name a few. Each section was charged with developing its own networks, plans, and strategies. In Denmark, a key SOE goal was to send in trained agents to organize and lead local sabotage actions. Why? Well, if the Danes could disrupt factories that supported the German war effort from inside Denmark itself, British planes would be freed up to focus on targets elsewhere.

Denmark wasn't the highest priority for SOE work. In the course of the war, while four hundred or so agents were deployed to Norway, which had more strategic German naval bases, only fifty-seven were sent to Denmark, all but one being

Danish. The work was hazardous. By the end of the war, thirty of the fifty-seven agents sent to Denmark had been evacuated, captured, or killed.

Denmark was part of the Scandinavian branch of the SOE, headed by Sir Charles Hambro. In late October 1940, Hambro went to Sweden to lay the groundwork for resistance efforts. In Stockholm, Sweden, he made arrangements with the British embassy to secretly house some SOE operations there. He also met with an influential Danish anti-Nazi journalist named Ebbe Munck. Munck agreed to help serve as a source of intelligence about Denmark. Munck had good connections with military intelligence officers in Denmark and would establish himself as a key contact between the burgeoning underground movement in Denmark and the outside world.

Everyone involved realized the road ahead would be long and hard; success wouldn't happen overnight. Reporting on his first meetings with Hambro during the fall of 1940, Munck said, "'Sir Charles was perfectly well aware of the fact that it would take some time before the Danish mentality was adjusted to the thought of sabotage, that it must necessarily take even longer before organizations with sufficient striking power were built up, properly manned and supplied with enough of the required sabotage material. But on broad lines, it was agreed, that we should work towards this goal.'"

British officials felt that the SOE should take on the role of coordinating sabotage targets and activity. Hambro had brought this up when he spoke with Munck: "'I made it clear at that time that it would not be in the interests of Denmark or

Great Britain, if uncoordinated sabotage was to break out in Denmark at the moment.'"

● ● ●

We might imagine that organizing resistance in an entire country would require a large staff. But in 1940, the Danish section of the SOE began with a core of just two men: Ralph Hollingworth in London and Ronald Turnbull in Stockholm.

The London SOE office was based at 62 Baker Street, near the fictional home of Sherlock Holmes (and a short walk from the Sherlock Holmes Museum today). This led to another nickname for the SOE: the Baker Street Irregulars, after the street children who appear in Sir Arthur Conan Doyle's stories as helpers to the famous detective.

Ralph Hollingworth faced a daunting task. Even the most basic requirements for a successful effort in Denmark were missing: access to radios to make regular contact with British officials, trained agents on the ground, and a system for dropping supplies and explosives for organized sabotage. An effective resistance movement would also need a solid plan of action and accurate information about potential targets.

Communication was a major stumbling block. Today individuals can use email, cell phones, and social media to communicate. Not so in the early 1940s. Just as it was difficult for Danes to get information about what was happening in the outside world, it was hard for their British allies to find out about the situation inside Denmark. That communication gap would take a long time—and lives lost—to try to close.

CHAPTER FOUR

Ralph had to start somewhere though. "'My orders from Hambro were, quite tersely, that I was to tackle the problem and get some results. How it was to be done, it was up to me to find out. . . . So we began studying methods in underground warfare, investigating how people elsewhere in similar circumstances had tackled things. At the same time we followed as far as we could, what was going on in Denmark . . . (gradually) we began, little by little, to get hold of certain ideas about what should be done, but . . . at the beginning we had the feeling that we were absolutely down to bed rock and left to our own devices.

"'I still remember . . . the two empty trays for outgoing and incoming correspondence, and a certain feeling of loneliness.'"

And so, sitting alone in his little office, Ralph Hollingworth tried to come up with a plan to help an entire country.

CHAPTER FIVE
FLIGHT OF THE HORNET

All Tommy Sneum needed was to get his hands on a plane.

He'd risked his life to get footage of Germany's new secret weapon: Freya radar. Now he was determined to get that information into the hands of the British by flying to Great Britain himself. Tommy's plan was daring—foolhardy even. But if anyone could make it work, he could.

Using his flying contacts, Tommy tracked down a farmer named Poul Andersen who lived on Fyn (Denmark's third largest island, connected to its largest and most populated island, Zealand, by a bridge). Andersen's farm had been the base of an aerial photographer before the war; rumor had it that Andersen still owned an old, small biplane, a model known as a de Havilland Hornet Moth.

Tommy first asked Andersen if he could buy the aircraft from him. Andersen refused. Tommy hesitated and then took a chance. "'Sir . . . what would your answer be if I told you the plane would go west?'"

Andersen grasped Tommy's meaning right away. The plane would head to Great Britain on some secret mission opposing the Germans. "'Then she's yours.'"

Later, as he stood in Andersen's barn looking at a jumble of scattered parts, Tommy couldn't help wondering if this particular plane would ever make it into the sky again. The tail fin, which had already been repaired once before, was stored in a crate, its condition unknown. The fuselage lay on the floor, the dusty wings in a corner. Tommy spotted a bag of bolts. Who knew if all the bolts needed to reattach the wings and tail fin were there? At least, Andersen had assured him, the engine was in good condition.

Reassembling an airplane wasn't the only problem with Tommy's scheme. The Hornet was a small two-seater with a maximum range of about 600 kilometers, or 372 miles. That meant England was beyond the Hornet's range on one tank of fuel. Since the route lay over the North Sea, there would be no place to land in order to refuel.

Scanning the barn, Tommy happened to spot two huge fuel drums. Andersen confirmed they were full. There was enough fuel to get to England. That gave Tommy an idea: What if he could refuel midflight over the North Sea?

For his part, Andersen didn't ask any questions about Tommy's plans and made it clear he didn't want to know details. (Tommy had also given him a false name as an extra precaution.) It was safer that way.

He told Tommy, "'I don't want to hear from you until you know what night you're leaving. On that particular night, I intend to be seen by as many witnesses as I can find, as far away from here as possible. And one other thing . . . if you're caught in my hangar in the meantime, I'll say you're a thief and claim I've never met you. I have a family to protect, you understand.'"

Fair enough. Still, getting the Hornet back together—and flying it across the North Sea—was too much for one man alone. Tommy would need help. Back in Copenhagen, he tracked down a friend and former pilot named Kjeld Pedersen and announced that they were flying to England.

Pedersen was game. " 'Are they sending a plane?' "

Not exactly, Tommy explained. They'd be fixing one up and flying it themselves to deliver crucial intelligence to the British. When Tommy told Pedersen he'd found a Hornet Moth, his friend laughed. " 'What? You want to fly to England in a Moth? It hasn't got the range . . .'

" 'I think it can be done. . . . We can refuel.' "

Pedersen was skeptical. " 'Just land in the North Sea and take off again? It isn't a seaplane, you know.'

"Sneum looked his friend in the eye. 'We'll do it in mid-air.'

"Pedersen's mouth dropped open. 'Now I know you're mad.' "

• • •

In the end, Kjeld Pedersen couldn't pass up the chance to be part of Tommy's audacious scheme. The next step was to return to the barn to examine the plane more closely. To avoid being seen by passing German patrols, they walked to the farm after nightfall from the nearest town, creeping across the turnip field in the darkness. They snuck into the barn, where they waited until daylight to examine their prize.

The wings looked in perfect shape. There was bad news though. After sorting through the bolts in the bag, they discovered that the ones needed to attach the wings to the fuselage were missing. They'd have to get some specially made through mechanics they knew.

Meanwhile, Tommy had been mulling over the problem of how to refuel. The large drums of fuel wouldn't work, as they were too large to store in the cockpit. They'd need to get some small fuel cans. And as for the dangerous refueling

CHAPTER FIVE

itself, no matter how much he thought about it, Tommy always came to the same conclusion: Someone would have to walk out on the wings of the plane over the open sea to reach the fuel tank.

He couldn't ask his friend to take that kind of risk. He would do it himself.

• • •

The two former pilots set to work. They tracked down mechanics they knew from their time in the Danish military and brought them to the hangar one night. The next morning, this volunteer crew worked silently to clean the Hornet's carburetor, check out the wiring, and change the oil. They reattached the Hornet's wings as best they could using the new bolts they'd arranged for other friends to make. Tommy also had sixteen fuel cans specially designed. Four could hold two gallons, and twelve were big enough to carry a gallon and a half of fuel each.

Tommy and Pedersen labored for weeks to get the plane ready for the dangerous flight. The spring days lengthened; the long hours of sunlight made secrecy more difficult. They took extra precautions not to be seen by farm laborers or passing patrols. Secrecy was essential: They didn't dare start the engine to test it, because the chances of someone hearing the noise and investigating were too high.

Slowly the Hornet began to look like an airworthy plane again. Tommy and Pedersen said their good-byes to family and trusted friends, warned the plane's owner, and then it was time. They were set to go.

Saturday, June 21, 1941, 11:00 p.m.

Tommy's daring mission wasn't going so well. For starters, he and Kjeld Pedersen couldn't even get the plane out of the barn! It had most likely been put into storage already dismantled. Now, as they quickly discovered, the doorway wasn't wide enough for it to pass through. It was a crucial detail they'd somehow missed.

The minutes ticked by. Tommy had planned their takeoff to coincide precisely with the local train schedule. There was a good reason for this. The rumble of the train would mask the sound of a plane engine roaring to life at midnight and lessen their chance of being discovered by a German patrol.

There was only one thing to do. Grabbing axes from the barn, Tommy and Pedersen cut space on the side of the barn doors to make room for the wings, working as quietly as they could. Soon they were sweating so much they slipped off their life jackets, which they'd put on to get ready for their overseas flight. "'Little by little, we managed to cut the plane free; and by pulling and pushing, after about fifteen minutes, we finally got it outside, though we heard a tearing sound at the last moment.'"

Part of the canvas covering on one wing had torn, but luckily the plywood underneath remained sound. Tommy thought the Hornet would still be fit. He'd have to trust his past training and instincts. He hadn't flown in more than a year, since the day all Danish planes had been grounded after the Nazi invasion. Pedersen was equally out of practice.

"'Can we make it?'" Pedersen wanted to know.

"'Of course we'll make it.'" Tommy tried to be optimistic. He climbed into the cockpit and checked his surroundings. He'd packed the cans of extra fuel, his precious rolls of film of the Freya radar, grape soda, biscuits, spare shirts, and something else—a broom handle with a white towel nailed to it. They didn't want to be mistaken for the enemy when they landed in England.

As for pinpointing their landing, they hadn't prepared quite so well in that department. "'Our only map of England was one we had torn from an atlas,'" Tommy admitted later.

The two young men heard the midnight train chugging in the distance. "'Contact!'" Tommy gave the order to turn the propeller, Pedersen gave a mighty push, and the engine burst to life.

Pedersen ran beside to help guide the Hornet through the turnip rows to reach a grassy field that would serve as a runway. Clouds of dust flew up, almost blinding Tommy. Then, when Pedersen finally jumped into the copilot seat, the broomstick blocked his way. As he pulled at it, the handle shot straight through the roof of the cockpit, tearing a ragged hole. They'd have a cold wind on their necks through the whole flight—if they ever got off the ground.

As they hurtled toward the train tracks, Tommy tried to take off. The little plane was weighted down by its heavy load of extra fuel. Several times he got the Hornet airborne, only to have it bounce back down to the ground again. High-voltage cables loomed ahead. Then an embankment. Then the railway tracks.

They *should* have been flying above those wires. But when Tommy finally felt the little plane lift into the air, he realized there wasn't enough time to clear the cables. He'd have to pull off an incredible stunt: Fly underneath.

"'I had to go down, keep the engine running full speed and try not to climb.'" Miraculously they sailed through—now only the hill and the train loomed before them.

Beside him, Pedersen screamed, "'Up! Up!'"

They were so close they could see the men driving the train, who must have been astonished at the sight of a small plane launching itself right at them. "'They were looking as though we had just fallen down from the moon,'" recalled Tommy.

Then they were above the train, still in one piece, flying toward freedom.

THE LITTLE PLANE
AND THE COLD, DARK SEA

" 'How is she flying . . . ?' " Kjeld Pedersen hollered to Tommy Sneum above the noise of the engine.

The answer wasn't reassuring. " 'The left wing feels twice as heavy as the right, everything is out of alignment, the nose pulls down and she seems to have a life of her own.' "

Still, Tommy was managing to keep the Hornet steady. If the two friends hoped the worst was over, they were in for a few surprises. First, the plane's compass was unreliable. When Tommy checked it against the railway tracks below, it seemed about thirty degrees off. Then there was that torn wing fabric, which made one wing feel twice as heavy as the other. Freezing air blowing down on them from the hole in the roof just added to their discomfort.

To lessen the risk of being spotted by the Germans, Tommy followed a zigzag pattern to make their flight look random and help disguise the fact they were heading west. It was tense inside the cockpit. A combination of the cold, blasting air, the twisting and turning, and perhaps a touch of nerves made Pedersen vomit. When they hit some heavy cloud cover, Tommy had to admit he wasn't sure exactly where they were.

All at once they were under attack. " 'Puffs of black smoke were exploding all around us from shellfire. . . . And tracer bullets seemed to be coming directly at us from below.' "

THE LITTLE PLANE AND THE COLD, DARK SEA

The cloud cover broke. Tommy got a glimpse of landmarks below and realized he was too far north. The path he'd wanted would have kept them away from German gun installations. Instead, they were over the northern tip of Fanø—close to the very radar tracking system he'd discovered.

The Nazis had the little plane in sight and were trying to blast it out of the sky. "'Up, up!'" Pedersen shouted once again.

Tommy didn't need urging. He wanted to avoid a direct hit. He pointed the Hornet's nose up and began to climb as steeply as he could, looking for more cloud cover.

Tense minutes passed. Miraculously no hit came. Tommy kept heading west. Suddenly they were in the clear. They'd somehow managed to shake off their pursuers.

"'There was an opening in the clouds and we saw the North Star right on the starboard side. I was so happy. It meant we were on the right course, flying due west, and we both knew it immediately.'"

...

The little plane buzzed along through the night, bringing the two Danes closer to their goal with every minute. But an hour or so into the flight, the reassuring hum of the engine unexpectedly fell silent, cutting out without warning.

"'No words will ever convey the sheer terror we felt during the following minutes . . . but we didn't panic,'" Tommy said, remembering that terrifying moment.

The engine sputtered back to life with a horrible clanking

In December 1943, the Germans shot down an English plane that was carrying SOE agents from Britain into Denmark; fortunately, all onboard survived.

sound, yet it was clear something was wrong. Desperately trying to troubleshoot, Tommy made a rapid check of the instrument panel and started gliding toward the water. They might have to make an emergency landing.

"'Find the life jackets,'" Tommy told Pedersen urgently, even though both knew their chances of surviving long in the North Sea were slim to none. At the very least, they could try to stay afloat on a piece of the plane and hope they'd be spotted.

Pedersen searched. No life jackets. That's when the awful truth struck: In the rush to take off, they'd left them by the barn door. A foolish mistake. "'We were both positive it spelled the end. We said goodbye and thanked each other for our friendship, which had stood the test of time, especially since the German invasion. The flight had been the toughest test of that friendship, because it is one thing to live together as pals, and another to die together,'" said Tommy.

With the engine cutting in and out, Tommy continued to drop altitude, bringing the little plane closer to the dark, churning sea. If he had to land, he wanted to try to set the aircraft down gently. All at once he heard a welcome, comforting sound. The Hornet's engine purred into life once more.

"'The plane suddenly seemed light as a feather and rose like an angel to five hundred meters. . . . I could hear solid lumps of things the size of eggs coming loose and clanking against the exhaust. That must have been chunks of ice.'"

Ice: so that was the culprit! Tommy realized he'd need to fly lower to avoid a deadly buildup of ice on the engine from happening again.

THE LITTLE PLANE AND THE COLD, DARK SEA

Another hurdle had been cleared, but the two friends had no time to "sit back and enjoy" this flight. Fuel was getting low. The moment had come for the most dangerous part of Tommy's plan: walking onto the wings to reach the fuel tank.

Tommy would have to perform the maneuver without a life jacket. Meanwhile, Pedersen, who also hadn't flown since leaving the military, would be on the spot. His job would be to keep the Hornet as steady as possible from the copilot's seat. Any quick jerk or jolt could throw Tommy off into the unforgiving waters below.

Pedersen gave Tommy some helpful advice: " 'Don't fall down.'

" 'Thanks, Pedersen,' Tommy replied. 'That was just what I needed to hear.' "

Tommy stuck his head out the door. " 'The wind was howling and it was pretty dark, because you couldn't see much in the thick fog. It was very cold and in those seconds the full reality and the great danger involved in going out there became clear. I was afraid of getting out. . . . I stepped out onto the wing with my right foot and held on to the inside of the doorframe with my left hand.' "

The plane banked a little, and Tommy felt grateful he was still partly inside. " 'I think we were about a hundred to a hundred and fifty meters above the sea. . . . But it didn't matter if we were a kilometer up in the sky or twenty meters. If I fell off, I'd had it.' "

Hose in hand and struggling to breathe in the frosty air, Tommy made his way back and fought to unscrew the fuel cap. "'At first I couldn't do it because my fingers were so numb, and I almost lost my balance.'"

He tried again. Then he had it! Next he needed to stick the hose into the fuel tank deep enough that it wouldn't become dislodged. The hose ran all the way to the cockpit, which would enable them to use a funnel and refuel from inside. "'I struggled to bend the hose down into the fuel tank. It felt so heavy all of a sudden, and I was dizzy and tired.'"

Somehow Tommy got it done. Shivering, he edged slowly back toward the front of the plane. He teetered precariously, nearly toppling into the darkness. With one final burst of effort, he wrenched the cockpit door open and lunged in, tumbling down nearly on top of his friend.

Tommy caught his breath. Inserting a funnel into the end of the hose, they began the process of refueling, pouring fuel from one can after another into a funnel stuck into the hose. It wasn't easy. "'Kjeld was spilling as much petrol down my back as was going into the tank. As it evaporated I felt colder still. I was covered in petrol. And the stench was overpowering.'"

The fumes were so bad that Pedersen became nauseous again and almost passed out. After forty-five minutes of work they managed to get most of the fuel through the hose. Now they just had to hope they didn't have to make a crash landing in England. The amount of fuel they'd spilled would definitely cause the little plane to burst into flames.

The rest of that long night was a struggle. A struggle to stay awake, to remain alert, to keep on course. Toward dawn, they began scanning the horizon, hoping for that first glimpse of land. Once, around 4:30 a.m., Pedersen was almost sure he spotted something. It turned out to be a trick of the fog. Then, just after dawn, they spied a white lighthouse gleaming against black rocky cliffs. Land at last.

That's when Tommy realized they weren't alone in the sky. Any unidentified plane in wartime was bound to arouse suspicion. The British had sent up four fighter planes to investigate. As for that white towel to prove their peaceful intentions? Forget that! They'd left it outside for much of the journey. The wind had battered it into a small, dirty cloth.

A Spitfire came close, and Tommy and Pedersen waved at the pilot. They could see him pointing downward. The message was clear: Land now!

Tommy spotted a field that looked smooth, a perfect landing spot. Suddenly it started to move. " 'The field came alive and I realized the smooth-looking surface I had identified was covered in sheep.' "

The landing was turning out to be almost as challenging as the takeoff. At last, avoiding a set of telephone wires, Tommy managed to bring the Hornet down in a cornfield (luckily the corn wasn't high yet), pulling up to a stop just before rolling onto a road.

It was 5:30 a.m. on Sunday, June 22, 1941. They'd been airborne for six hours and five minutes of continuous flight in a single-engine aircraft. Tommy wasn't thinking about their achievement. " 'We were just happy to be alive.' "

The two eager young Danes were stiff and sore, but they moved as fast as they could. Tommy said, " 'We had fresh white shirts and uniform jackets folded behind our seats, and in our jacket pocket we each had a tie, which we proceeded to put on. We wanted to be presentable, so that we would be treated like gentlemen.'"

Soon vehicles from a nearby airbase pulled up and the Danes identified themselves. "'Flight Lieutenants Sneum and Pedersen, Danish Fleet Air Arm, at your service. . . . We're here to help you fight Hitler. We've just flown across the North Sea.'"

"'In that?'" One British officer looked skeptically at the two men, and then at their tiny plane in the cornfield. "'Not a chance.'"

UPS AND DOWNS
IN THE LIFE OF A SPY

If Tommy Sneum had imagined getting a hero's welcome in Great Britain, he was about to be sadly disappointed.

Within minutes of landing, he handed over his precious films of the secret Freya radar. Then Tommy and Kjeld Pedersen were whisked off to a nearby military base, never to see the little Hornet again. Interrogations began that day. The next morning the two were sent to London for further questioning. They were being treated as illegal aliens since they hadn't come into the country through normal channels.

Tommy realized their situation was serious. The British suspected them of being German spies. If he couldn't convince them otherwise, he and Pedersen might end up spending the rest of the war in an internment camp.

"'I was aware, as I told them the story of my escape yet again, that it didn't sound very likely,'" Tommy said. "'They didn't believe what I was saying, at least some of them didn't, even though they had RAF backgrounds themselves. Perhaps that was the very reason they didn't believe me, because they hadn't heard of such a thing being done before, especially not in a Hornet Moth. They said it was all lies. But what could I do? I just told them the truth again and again. . . . I kept asking . . . when my films would be back from their laboratory, because I thought that when they saw the quality of those images, it would end the argument.'"

CHAPTER SEVEN

Then Tommy got some heartbreaking news. His films had been processed incorrectly and badly damaged. "'I went mad when I realized what had happened.'"

Tommy couldn't help lashing out at the British intelligence officers. "'Do you know how many times I risked my life for those films?'"

Two experts were called in to examine what was left of the footage. Despite the damage, Reginald Victor Jones, head of Scientific Intelligence, was able to make sense of some images. Maybe he could be persuaded to believe Tommy's incredible tale.

Tommy recounted again all his efforts to capture what he'd seen, and how he'd witnessed the equipment moving as it tracked an incoming aircraft. Said Tommy: "'They could see what it was but they couldn't really make out the detail because of the damage done, so I tried to explain what was shown. I wasn't an expert but he made me feel like I was. Then we noticed a few clearly definable images. It was an exciting moment, and the scientists eagerly went to work.'"

By tracing the images on paper, the experts were able to detect the equipment's revolving action. Jones finally seemed willing to confirm Tommy's story. "'Freya radar. . . . Hitler's latest defense system. We've seen aerial photographs of these things from France. But we didn't know the Germans were using this type of radar in Denmark. . . .

"'These are the first pictures I've seen of Freya taken on the ground,' Jones purred. 'Moving pictures, that's a first too. Imagine what he had to go through to get them.'"

Jones now had no doubts about Tommy. "'Gentlemen, . . . I think we have to accept that what we have here is not a double-agent but a man who has demonstrated bravery of the highest order.'"

Later, Jones wrote that he could appreciate Tommy's indignation at his treatment and the inept handling of the images, which were, after all, "'the sole relics of a gallant exploit. . . . Not only had he and his friend risked their lives several times over, but also they had brought with them very valuable information only to have it ruined. . . . At the same time, there was an almost inevitable irony about such episodes, because the more gallant and therefore improbable they were, the harder it was to believe that they had really happened.'"

Hard to believe, but true. Tommy had succeeded in his seemingly impossible quest. He had flown a small plane across the sea to smuggle crucial intelligence out of Denmark.

· · ·

A few days later Tommy Sneum and Kjeld Pedersen were officially cleared of suspicion. What next? They wanted to join Britain's Royal Air Force to help in the war effort. Tommy even proposed that the British try to get more Danish aviators out of Denmark to join the fight in the air. British military officials in the Secret Intelligence Service (SIS, sometimes called MI6), however, had a different job in mind. They wanted the two to return to Denmark as intelligence agents.

Pedersen balked at the request. He had no wish to go back and convinced the British to let him fly instead. Although

CHAPTER SEVEN

he still wanted to be a war pilot, Tommy found himself agreeing to the plan. "'I answered that only one of us could do it, because we were probably hunted as a pair, wanted men together, and that I would like to be the one to go back because I already had so many useful connections for such a job.'"

Tommy Sneum had just barely managed to escape the Nazis. Now he would be going back as Great Britain's first wartime spy in Denmark.

CHAPTER EIGHT
RENEGADE: A SABOTEUR IN ACTION

Since that first autumn night when he'd crossed the line from student to saboteur, Niels Skov had been acting alone. When he returned to his hometown of Ribe during the Christmas holidays of 1940, resistance to the occupation was uppermost on his mind. A good childhood friend, Aage Kjellerup, met him at the train station.

Niels wanted to share his commitment but couldn't be sure exactly where Kjellerup stood. Was it safe to talk about what he'd been doing? Niels knew some Danes were pro-German, and many simply didn't feel comfortable doing anything to disrupt the fragile situation. He began casually questioning his friend about the Germans in town.

Niels asked, "'Has anyone bothered them?'

"'What do you mean?'"

Niels threw out a list of possible resistance actions—slashing tires, acting unfriendly, tampering with the Germans' food supply. No, that wasn't happening, Kjellerup told him. In fact, it was just the opposite: The townspeople had been relatively friendly and collaborative toward the Germans. Then Kjellerup asked the question Niels had hoped to hear: "'But what can we do?'"

Niels chose his words carefully. "'As I see it, Denmark took a pitiful position when we knuckled down on the 9th of April. Some of the other countries have been intimidated by the Germans too, but the Danes are at the bottom. And that goes for you and me whether we like it or not. Now, we can sit and wait for the English and French to get us out of this pickle, but we ought to do something about it ourselves as well.'"

"'Are you saying we should try to kill some Germans?'" Kjellerup wanted to know.

Niels pondered the question as they walked along. "'No. I think our careers would be too short if we tried, but we can get away with something else that will hurt them a little. I know. . . . Because I have been doing it. And it's not difficult.'"

Kjellerup let out a low whistle. "'Tell me about it.'"

- - -

The two friends talked late into the night. They didn't want to harm anyone by their actions. Instead, their goal was to take a stand and make a powerful, public statement by targeting property being controlled by the Nazis. Niels Skov and his new recruit didn't waste any time putting their partnership into action. A few nights later they set out for a building where the Germans were storing supplies.

Niels described the scene. "Aage had placed himself at the corner of the garage building. . . . A snowberry bush leaning over the fence covered him from a soldier standing guard at the main hotel entrance forty yards away, but the midnight darkness was in any event too deep to discern anyone at a distance of more than a few feet. The garage building was a small brick structure, holding four stalls facing the street, each closed with two hinged doors secured with a padlock."

While Aage Kjellerup kept watch, Niels approached the second stall, inserting a heavy screwdriver into the padlock to break the lock. Once inside he struck a match. It revealed a motorcycle and sidecar, a couple of bicycles—and a fuel can.

"I fumbled, found the fuel can and lifted it." No luck. It was empty. Striking another match, Niels located the motorbike again. His match went out, though not before he had located the bike's fuel tank.

"Under the tank I felt the fuel line; I drew the screwdriver from my belt and inserted it between the line and the tank. Striking one more match, I checked its position and leverage, blew out the match and slowly bore down on the screwdriver. The smell and feel of gasoline announced that a leak had been opened, and I stopped. A small trickle was best. Then I walked to the door in the dark, no more lighting matches. The outside darkness felt less intense, and the frosty air smelled good, I walked the few steps to Aage's position at the snowberry bush."

Niels whispered, "'All quiet?'

"'Yes. What do you find?'

"'A motorcycle. The fuel is dribbling out and ready to light, but you'd better do it, for my hands are soaked with gasoline. Here are the matches. We'll switch positions, and when it's lit, we run that way.'"

Opening the door slightly, Kjellerup could smell the gasoline. He cautioned, "'Phew, this is going to explode when I light it. Be ready to run.'" Striking two matches, he lit them and tossed them quickly into the garage.

"The fuel lit with a soft WHOOSH and momentarily illuminated a slice of snow-covered street. Then he pulled the door almost shut, and the two of us sprinted down the dark and silent street, our footsteps making no sound in the snow. After fifty yards we turned into a side street and started walking normally," said Niels.

...

Niels Skov and Aage Kjellerup were taking a grave risk. They were operating independently, without collaborating with any other organized group. They had limited knowledge of targets, no training, and no access to explosives. While they were dedicated in their commitment to defy the Germans, they also represented the lack of coordination the SOE's Sir Charles Hambro was hoping to avoid.

Back in his Baker Street office, Ralph Hollingworth had been working for months to develop an SOE road map for Danish resistance efforts. He also wanted to find, train, and deploy a chief organizer to help build a network of brave volunteers willing to perform dangerous acts of sabotage. In the fall of 1941, Ralph found the perfect candidate to lead the SOE's work in Denmark and began to plan his first operation.

Yet before Ralph could put his plans into action, something happened to confuse the situation. The SOE's rival intelligence agency, the British Secret Intelligence Service (SIS), had already found a man willing to be a British spy in Denmark. In other words, without consulting leaders of the new SOE, the more established SIS had gone ahead on its own.

And that SIS spy? Well, he might not have had much training, but he was resourceful, fearless, and willing to do just about anything for the cause. And he had dropped in at just the right time, from out of the sky.

That daredevil's name was, of course, Tommy Sneum.

SQUARE PEG IN A ROUND HOLE: THE SPY WHO DROPPED IN FROM THE COLD

Less than three months after his daring escape, Tommy Sneum went back to Denmark. His return in early September of 1941 turned out to be almost as treacherous as his flight out of the country.

Once again, the mission began in the air. And once again, Tommy wasn't alone. This time Tommy's partner was a young Dane named Sigfred Christophersen, who would serve as Tommy's assistant and radio operator. Christophersen had received a little training in Morse code from the British. His job would be to establish regular radio communications with Great Britain.

From the outset, the two men had problems working together. It was more than just a personality conflict. Tommy was concerned about Christophersen's readiness for the risks and dangers ahead. Christophersen had told him, " 'I'll do my bit, and a lot more. But if we get compromised, I want to survive.' "

Statements like that made Tommy nervous: Could Christophersen be trusted? Would he do whatever it took to protect his partner? Despite his doubts, the decision wasn't Tommy's to make. The SIS had selected Christophersen, and Tommy had no say in the matter.

Now the two were about to become the first British agents to be dropped secretly into Denmark by parachute. Tommy

The SOE dropped agents into Denmark by parachute during the occupation.

was ready to leap as soon as he saw Christophersen's parachute unfurl. But an adjustment had to be made to his line at the last minute. That meant the plane flew another half mile past the original drop spot. This would make it harder for the two men to find each other once they were on the ground.

Tommy flung himself out and struggled to breathe in the ice-cold air. He felt a reassuring wrench as the parachute opened and drifted slowly through the night.

All at once, he was in trouble. "'I felt something sharp tear into my legs and backside. . . . I then felt a terrible pain just above my buttocks. I thought I must have broken something, perhaps even my back, and I was worried I wouldn't be able to walk.'"

Tommy had crashed into a barbed wire fence. He struggled to get to his feet. He could walk, but just barely. Searing pains shot up his back. He guessed, correctly, that he'd damaged his coccyx (tailbone). "'It was excruciating work just to fold up the parachute. I'd never known anything like it.'"

Pain or not, Tommy had to get moving. Their orders were clear: Leave the drop site immediately. If the parachutes had been spotted, a patrol could be on its way and the whole area might be sealed off.

Tommy wanted to avoid being stopped if at all possible, though he did have a cover story ready just in case. He'd chosen to wear regular, everyday clothes and shoes. If challenged, Tommy would claim he'd been at a party and gotten into a fight over a girl—and had the cuts and bruises to prove it. (As it happens, that tale wasn't out of character. Tommy had a reputation as a ladies' man who loved to party.) He'd even brought a hip flask of cognac to make his story more believable.

Moving slowly, Tommy buried the parachute under a stump in the woods, covering it up with leaves. There was no sign of Christophersen. The two had agreed that if they became separated, they'd each get to Copenhagen and meet up the next day.

Tommy set out on the road but soon spotted a car's headlights. He dropped into some bushes, trying not to scream with pain when he had to move suddenly. The car passed slowly. As he peered into the darkness, Tommy realized it was the Danish police. "'That got me worried. We were in the middle of nowhere, so what was a patrol car doing out there?'" Had the white drifting parachutes been spotted?

Tommy kept on. Later he found that Christophersen hadn't obeyed orders to leave the spot immediately. Instead, Christophersen had hidden in the woods until dawn before making his way to Copenhagen—a breach of protocol that could have endangered both men if he'd been discovered.

In the early morning, Tommy found a taxi in a small town nearby. He persuaded the driver to take him all the way to Copenhagen, about an hour's drive. The driver was pleased at such a large fare. But when they arrived, Tommy reached into his pocket and discovered that he had only Swedish bills. Big mistake!

The driver insisted they stop at a train station so Tommy could exchange the Swedish currency for Danish. Tommy was worried. "'I thought . . . this is going to be dangerous—the railway station in Copenhagen was usually crawling with Germans.'"

Tommy knew he looked a sorry sight, limping along with dried bloodstains on his torn trousers. He was also carrying forged identity papers. "'My heart was pounding when I went up to an exchange counter, especially when I saw a doubtful expression on the face of the clerk. Even after I changed the money and began walking back toward the taxi, I thought I might feel a hand on my shoulder and hear the order to stop.'"

Tommy was able to meet up with Christophersen; he found the radio operator a safe place to stay with an old friend. Next, Tommy had to find out exactly what had been injured in the jump, because the pain in his back wasn't any better. Tommy went to see a man he could trust: Ole Chievitz, a professor of surgery who later became active in the Danish underground press. Chievitz confirmed that Tommy had cracked his coccyx, which fortunately would heal on its own. Tommy refused the offer of a hospital bed. He had more worries than just physical pain. He had a mission to run.

■ ■ ■

The rocky start of Tommy Sneum's return set the tone for the months ahead. Tommy spent his time trying to gather information about German activity in Denmark, such as factories that were part of the German war machine. Then he and Sigfred Christophersen would relay the information to the British on their radio. But he continued to worry about Christophersen's abilities as well as his casual approach to security. Tommy had other problems too—problems he himself didn't really understand.

The fact is that while Tommy had been recruited by the SIS, not by Ralph Hollingworth and the SOE, he himself wasn't aware of the differences between the two branches of British military intelligence. Tommy was an amateur who knew nothing of the political conflicts between the two agencies as to which would be in charge of activities in Denmark. He wasn't even sure of the name of the agency that had recruited him. About all Tommy knew was that he was helping the British.

As it happens, Tommy wasn't the only one confused about the internal workings of British intelligence. Soon after he arrived, Tommy contacted three top members of the Danish intelligence division of the Danish government, known by the nickname the Princes. Their names were Colonel Einar Nordentoft, Major Hans Lunding, and Captain Volmer Gyth. Up to this point, the Princes had been in touch with the SOE through two contacts in Stockholm: Ronald Turnbull and resistance sympathizer Ebbe Munck, the Danish journalist who had previously met with Sir Charles Hambro and agreed to serve as a contact between Denmark and the British. The Princes had begun to consider the SOE their partner in helping to build and coordinate resistance efforts within Denmark.

Turnbull felt the Princes could be helpful to the SOE and had described them to his boss, Ralph Hollingworth, this way: "'The Princes are . . . wonderfully placed for our work. They play in with the Germans and see and know all that is going on. . . . They are big men, therefore we cannot give them orders. We can let them know our suggestions, and we can find out from them their requirements. It seems therefore that my job is to act as liaison between you and them.' "

Great Britain couldn't just tell the Princes what to do in their own country. As one historian has put it: "It had to be a partnership between equals, and not one of subordination." The SOE knew the road ahead wouldn't always be easy; Turnbull said, "Even with the best will in the world, there are bound to be square pegs and round holes."

But that's exactly where Tommy found himself when he first tried to make contact with the Princes: a square peg trying to fit into a round hole. Tommy found himself caught in the middle of a sensitive, complex situation with nuances he couldn't appreciate.

From the point of view of the Princes, Tommy had simply come out of nowhere. They were naturally suspicious and upset. Who was this man? After all, *their* SOE British contacts hadn't informed them about Tommy. For all they knew, he could be a German spy.

And so when Tommy tried to make contact with the Princes, word came back through a third party that the Princes needed actual proof that he'd been dropped in by parachute. Tommy made a dangerous trip back to the countryside disguised as a landscape painter carrying canvas and paints. There he managed to find the parachute where he'd hidden it.

When Tommy was finally able to meet with the Princes, it didn't go well, since Tommy didn't understand the big picture and how he fit into it. He had no knowledge of the SOE and no way of knowing that the SOE was working to develop a cooperative relationship with the Princes.

Tommy must also have come across as arrogant. "'I told them I was serving directly with the British and that made me their superior. They told me I was talking nonsense because their rank was far superior. I wasn't going to accept that, not when they had done so little against the Nazis since the invasion. They had never taken the sort of risks I had taken, but they dared to question my loyalty.'"

Eventually tempers calmed and an uneasy relationship began. Tommy was offered a room in a safe house and, in return, promised to write a report for the Princes on his time in England and his flight on the Hornet so they would understand his background a bit better.

Still, Tommy's position was precarious. Nor was he getting much support from the SIS back in Britain. For instance, his SIS contact in London had given him the name of a banker to contact who was supposed to provide him money to live on. Tommy visited the man, saying the correct code phrase, "'Strange weather when you can't make biscuits.'" But the banker put him off, telling him to come back in a few weeks.

Despite these difficulties, throughout that fall Tommy did his best to communicate to the British anything he found out about German activities in Denmark. To help improve the team's radio transmissions, Sigfred Christophersen suggested they get in touch with a man his brother knew named Lorens Arne Duus Hansen. A brilliant radio engineer, Duus Hansen had the ability to design and build his own radio sets.

Hansen would turn out to be a key player in the Danish

resistance. Tommy said, " 'It was because Duus and I got on so well that I was lucky enough to be able to benefit from his help on a regular basis, and that led him to maintain his relationship with the British for the rest of the war.' "

Hansen invented a small radio set, "a spy's dream in Nazi-occupied Europe, more practical and effective than anything British experts had devised." He also worked on a high-speed transmission system, which made broadcasts quicker and reduced the chances of being detected by the Germans.

Thanks to Hansen, Tommy was able to send valuable information back to Great Britain. He reported the names of German intelligence officers in Copenhagen, details he'd gleaned about German ships and troop movements, sugges-

A telegraph being sent to London from Denmark on a radio transmitter developed by Duus Hansen.

tions for strategic targets such as factories or bridges, and names of the Danish police who seemed to be cooperating most closely with the Nazis. Through the university contacts of Ole Chievitz, the doctor who'd helped him when he'd been hurt in the parachute drop, Tommy was even beginning to investigate rumors related to Germany's potential to develop a nuclear bomb.

By December of 1941, Tommy had been working for the British SIS for three months. On Christmas Eve, as he stopped by a florist's shop to get flowers for his landlady, he noticed a woman staring at him. Tommy recognized her as the wife of a former military colleague. He also remembered that she was pro-German.

Tommy was wearing a pair of glasses and a false mustache, but he still might have been recognized. He'd have to take extra precautions not to be followed. The danger of being reported to the police by an informer was real, Tommy knew. "'I was afraid more often than people seem to realize. . . . Who wouldn't have been afraid?'"

In fact, Tommy's position was about to become even more precarious. Although Tommy couldn't know it, Ralph Hollingworth and the SOE were about to make their first move. But once again there would be trouble with parachutes, and new danger for anyone in Denmark suspected of being a spy.

CHAPTER TEN
A FLAME GOES OUT

Where is my bag? A green lady's handbag,
lock missing, lost . . .
          —*Politiken* newspaper ad, January 1, 1942

Just before midnight on December 27, 1941, the drone of a British plane could be heard in the cold skies over Denmark. If anyone had been awake to listen, that is. The houses below were still and dark in the winter night, their windows taped because of a blackout.

The pilots, though, were wide-awake as they searched for a small town called Haslev, less than fifty miles from Copenhagen. Behind them, four men huddled in the noisy cargo compartment of the plane. In just a short while, a recent medical school graduate named Dr. Carl Johan Bruhn, along with Mogens Hammer, a former member of the merchant navy who'd left his ship to volunteer in England, would be dropped by parachute into the forest below. Bruhn and Hammer were the first agents being sent in by the SOE.

Bruhn was a bright, dedicated young man with the ability to organize—the kind of leader Ralph Hollingworth and the SOE needed to establish a network of sabotage groups in Denmark. Bruhn would carry their most valuable piece of equipment: a wireless transmitter to set up ongoing radio communication with London. Hammer had recently been trained in Morse code to serve as a radio operator and to support Bruhn.

Carl Johan Bruhn.

There would be one other parachute, though it wouldn't drop a person. A metal container with explosive materials and supplies to be used for sabotage operations sat in the rear of the plane, ready to be flung out with the two agents. This was just the first load of material they'd need to begin large-scale sabotage actions against targets like factories supporting the German war machine.

Months of planning, training, and preparation had gone into the SOE's first operation. It was about to become a disaster.

• • •

In the long months since he'd taken charge of the Danish section of the SOE, Ralph Hollingworth had worked diligently to develop a thorough, meticulous operations plan. He called it BOOKLET. It had six separate parts, each named for a piece of furniture. All together, it was designed to provide a blueprint for an effective resistance effort in Denmark. The six areas of action were:

CHAIR—building a secret army within Denmark;
DRESSER—developing lines of communication;
SETTEE—a financial structure to fund local resistance operations;
CHEST—anti-German propaganda;
DIVAN—a special intelligence network;
TABLE—the effort to build sabotage groups within Denmark.

By December 15, 1941, Ralph had received official approval for his plan from SOE leaders. By then, preparations were well under way to launch the first project within TABLE, dropping two agents by parachute into Denmark to organize and recruit people to take part in sabotage.

As the plane rumbled through the sky to the drop site, Carl Bruhn must have felt a heavy weight of responsibility on his shoulders. The SOE had placed an enormous challenge before him: to disrupt and destroy the German war machine in Denmark. The SOE's goals included dividing Denmark into six regions of sabotage operations. Bruhn's job would be to recruit leaders for each area to develop trained, active sabotage groups of individuals willing to undertake this hazardous work.

Bruhn would also begin identifying potential sabotage targets—factories all over the country that were making everything from German weapons to uniforms. The SOE envisioned a coordinated effort—not at all like the homegrown sabotage Niels Skov and others were doing. Regular radio communications from Denmark to Great Britain would be used to share information about potential targets and arrange for the drop of explosives.

Ralph thought Bruhn would be perfect for this difficult job. In his mid-thirties, Bruhn had been born in Denmark. A love of adventure had taken him to Malaya, where he'd met and married an English doctor. When war broke out, Bruhn and his wife were living in London; he had gone back to school for a medical degree. A bright future awaited him. Yet he wanted to help his country. He'd volunteered and been selected for an SOE training program. Ralph called Bruhn "'a fine man, an idealist in all he undertook . . . a man of brilliant talents.'"

Bruhn and Hammer had been briefed on how to send a secret message to the SOE once they arrived, using a code placed in a newspaper advertisement. They were ready. All systems were go.

• • •

At about 3:00 a.m. on December 28, 1941, the bomber reached the drop zone near the town of Haslev, where Carl Bruhn had contacts who could help the two agents once they landed. The pilot dropped to about five hundred feet. Since Bruhn was lighter than Mogens Hammer, he'd been chosen to carry the radio set. Bruhn jumped first. Hammer followed close behind. The container with the explosives was tossed out right behind them.

CHAPTER TEN

From above, the pilots thought all went well. Although the dispatcher who gave the order for the men to jump thought there might have been a problem with one of the lines, the rear gunner was certain he saw three parachutes open. Once they were back in Britain, crew members reported a successful mission: The two agents, the radio set, and the sabotage material had all been dropped safely.

That's not what happened.

Carl Bruhn's parachute never opened. He hit the ground and was killed instantly. The radio set he carried on his back was completely destroyed.

"Bruhn's death was a catastrophe," wrote resistance historian Jørgen Hæstrup. "Not only did SOE lose the man they had chosen as the pioneer of the work, and in whose ability and character they had put such hopes, but in addition, Hammer found himself in a hopeless situation, so that the work in Denmark had a false start, with all the difficulties this dragged with it."

Mogens Hammer didn't leave a written account of that night, but he did tell his brother what happened next. Svend Erik Hammer remembered his brother's story this way: " 'When he landed, he hid his parachute in a ditch and immediately began to look for Bruhn, with whom he had arranged a particular whistle signal. However, he heard no sound, and it was only by chance that he found Bruhn lying dead. He had to search Bruhn at once. He knew that his friend had money hidden in his boots, and he had to cut them open.' "

Bruhn's body remained where he had fallen. The footsteps in the snow would tell the whole story to the Danish police and German military officials: Two British agents had been dropped by parachute. One had been killed. The other was on the loose, most likely in Copenhagen. But if the Nazis had their way, he wouldn't be free for long.

...

As light dawned on the morning of December 28, 1941, a shaken young man made his way out of the wintry forest toward the town of Haslev. Mogens Hammer was six feet tall, with broad shoulders and the body of an athlete. He'd been a Danish swimming champion before the war.

The original plan had gone something like this: Carl Bruhn knew several of the farmers in the area around Haslev. He would ask for their help in getting false identity papers and ration cards for food for both men. Then he and Hammer would get settled in Copenhagen and try to make contact with like-minded people willing to work against the Germans.

Secrecy would be key to the agents' success. They knew German patrols had equipment that could detect illegal radio transmissions. They'd need to move around frequently and find people willing to let their apartments be used for this dangerous activity. Before they left London, the SOE's Ralph Hollingworth had given Bruhn some names to contact to help with this part of the operation.

All the plans had been well thought out—up to a certain point. There was no plan B. No one had anticipated Bruhn's death. The element of surprise was blown. Hammer hadn't been trained to fill Bruhn's shoes. He wasn't an experienced agent, or even a soldier. He was a young man completely on his own.

It can't have been easy for Hammer to cut away Bruhn's boots to retrieve the money hidden inside. But he did. Then he followed the railway lines until he could get on a train. Hammer knew that both the Danish police and German soldiers would be looking for him. Even if he'd been able to hide his parachute, his footsteps in the snow would be proof that two agents had arrived and one was still alive.

In fact, within days after the tragedy at Haslev, the Germans sent a note to the Danish police asking for their help in finding the surviving parachute agent. They'd been put on alert and would be watching for more secret drops. College student Jørgen Kieler recalled reading an article in a newspaper a few weeks later, calling for any information leading to the spy's arrest. There was even the promise of a reward.

Mogens Hammer was most definitely a wanted man.

■ ■ ■

Given the danger from possible informants, the last thing Mogens Hammer should have done is contact people he knew. Doing so might put them in danger. But with nowhere else to turn, Hammer had no choice: He needed a place to sleep. He didn't let on the actual truth: that he had left the Danish merchant navy when his boat docked in Great Britain and volunteered to help his country. Instead, he made up a story about his sudden reappearance, telling friends and family he'd been shipwrecked and had managed to make his way to Denmark through Sweden.

Mogens Hammer.

CHAPTER TEN

Next, Hammer went looking for help to find other like-minded people involved in secret resistance efforts. His path took him to a newspaper editor named Erik Seidenfaden.

"'One fine day, a stranger rang at my door. He introduced himself as Mr. Hansen, and asked to speak with me. I was alone at home and asked him in, and he at once put his cards on the table, told me that he was a British agent, that he had just landed near Haslev,'" Seidenfaden recalled later. "'We had a long talk, and he seemed to take it for granted that I had contacts which I did not have.'"

Even as Hammer struggled to find his way, the Germans and the Danish police went on the alert, watching for signs of radio activity or of anyone acting suspicious. Things weren't looking good for the start of the SOE's efforts to build an effective sabotage organization.

Things weren't going much better for the other British spy in Denmark: Tommy Sneum.

THE NOOSE TIGHTENS

Tommy Sneum was beginning to worry. First there'd been that scare on Christmas Eve, when he might have been recognized by a possible pro-German informant. Then, in January, Tommy got a call from a police friend who had unsettling news: A fellow policeman had started asking about Tommy's whereabouts.

Had he been found out? Had a German sympathizer made a report about him to the authorities? Or did the Danish police and the Germans suspect Tommy might be the missing agent who had parachuted in at Haslev?

Tommy simply couldn't be sure if his cover was blown. As a precaution, he decided to lie low for a while and get his groceries delivered. If the police were looking for him he didn't want to increase the risk of being recognized by chance at local shops. Luckily he'd finally been able to get some money from the banker whose name the SIS had given him, so at least he could buy food.

One day, when the delivery boy brought supplies, Tommy paid him by taking cash from a pocket in his coat that was hanging by the door. Tommy turned his back for a few minutes to put something away. In that instant, the boy slipped his hand into the pocket, hoping to find more money. Instead, he discovered a gun.

Tommy didn't miss the gun until hours later. He searched his whole apartment before he realized what must have happened. Tommy figured it would be only a matter of hours before the young thief would begin bragging that he'd found a gun. The police were sure to hear about it. They would then investigate, as any private citizen owning a gun was suspected of being involved in the resistance.

That's exactly what happened. That very afternoon, the delivery boy fired a few shots to impress his friends. Confronted by police officers, he admitted he'd stolen the gun and gave them Tommy's address. Tommy was now in grave danger.

As soon as he'd realized the weapon was missing, Tommy had called radio operator Lorens Arne Duus Hansen and Kaj Oxlund, an old friend from his military days, who'd been helping him gather information about German activities. Hansen and Oxlund could be trusted. Tommy needed to get away from the apartment—and fast. His friends arrived to carry away his belongings, each leaving separately with a bag.

Tommy still had the most damaging piece of evidence: a valuable radio set Hansen had built. Being caught with it meant certain arrest. Tommy let the others get clear. Before he could leave with the radio, his landlady called with a warning: Two men were approaching the house.

It was too late to try to escape out the window. The men were soon outside his door. His landlady, a resistance sympathizer, was doing her best to distract the two plainclothesmen, telling them her tenant had gone out at lunch and hadn't returned.

"'Do you have a spare key?'" asked one of the officers. "'Otherwise I'm afraid we'll have to break down the door.'"

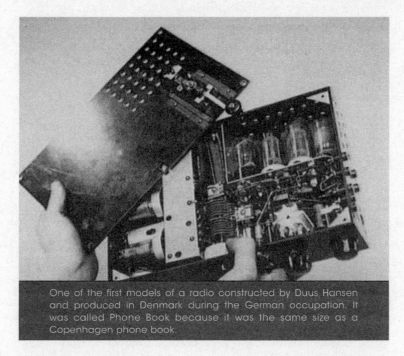

One of the first models of a radio constructed by Duus Hansen and produced in Denmark during the German occupation. It was called Phone Book because it was the same size as a Copenhagen phone book.

Thinking fast, the landlady invited the police officers into her apartment to look for a duplicate key, speaking loudly enough that Tommy could hear from where he stood, heart pounding, on the other side of the door. She said, "'You can see the street from there, so you will be in a good position to notice when he comes home. Follow me.'"

Tommy waited a moment. When he guessed the coast was clear, he grabbed the radio and slipped silently down the stairs. On the street, he turned in the opposite direction from the window where the policemen were waiting while the land-lady searched for a spare key as slowly as she could, trying to stall for time. Tommy was able to make his way to Oxlund's apartment, where he placed the precious radio set in a hid-ing place under the floorboards.

CHAPTER ELEVEN

Tommy now had to find a new place to live. For a while he stayed in the cellar of one of his professor friends, but the man felt the risk to his family was too high. Anyone suspected of helping the resistance could be arrested. Tommy ended up moving into Oxlund's apartment, where radio operator Sigfred Christophersen was also staying.

But Tommy felt nervous there. The situation didn't feel secure. The building caretaker always seemed to be watching them, especially when they left with the box containing the radio transmitter. It seemed that any day now the man would decide to share his suspicions with the police.

Tommy remained concerned that Christophersen was still not taking security seriously. Afraid that their whole mission would unravel, Tommy decided that Christophersen should go. He faked a message from Great Britain ordering him to pull out.

Christophersen made plans to escape over the ice to Sweden, along with his brother and Oxlund, who was also increasingly anxious about getting caught. The three set out to make the dangerous crossing to Sweden in early March. It turned out to be a tragic undertaking. They encountered weak ice and all fell through. They were able to pull them-selves out and keep going. Yet in the end, only Christophersen survived the ordeal. The other two men died of exposure before they could reach safety.

After Oxlund's body was identified, the Danish police began asking questions of the neighbors in the apartment building where he and Christophersen had lived with Tommy. Everyone involved in the fledgling Danish resistance efforts was nervous. There were other repercussions as well.

One of the Princes arranged a secret meeting in Stockholm with the SOE's Ronald Turnbull. The result was a closer alliance between Danish intelligence and the SOE. Back in London, the SIS agreed that from this point on, the SOE would be the only British intelligence branch involved in Denmark. Tommy, of course, wasn't working for the SOE but for SIS. It was now increasingly clear that Tommy could no longer be effective.

The Princes summoned Tommy to a meeting and told him he must leave. To make matters worse, Tommy had been spotted in the company of German officers, which added to their distrust. Tommy tried to explain that this was part of his method. By pretending to be a sympathizer, he was able to collect valuable information.

His arguments went nowhere. The Princes wanted him out. They assured him that if he were picked up by the Swedes, he wouldn't be turned over to the Germans as a spy. He would be released and then be free to contact the British legation in Stockholm and get to England. One of the Princes told him: " 'Sneum, you have my word of honor as a gentleman. The deal with the Swedes has been done. You just have to put together another plan to escape from Denmark.' "

As Tommy made preparations to leave, he tried to ensure that the work he'd begun would continue. He urged the brilliant radio operator Duus Hansen to stay involved and make contact with Mogens Hammer, the SOE agent who'd survived the parachute accident.

Hansen agreed. Later he said, " 'We had tried to get in contact with Hammer without success, and it was a deal between Sneum and me that I should do everything to get in contact and achieve a successful working relationship with this man, which I managed to do.' "

. . .

Tommy's days as a spy were over. Now he needed to escape to Sweden—across the same frozen ice that had just killed two others.

Tommy would not make the dangerous crossing to Sweden alone, but with another resistance activist named Arne Helvard. Helvard had been working at an airport in Denmark, where he gathered information about German airplanes and anti-aircraft artillery. He also felt in danger of arrest.

On March 26, 1942, the two men met in the city's central railway station and took a train north to Skodsborg, a coastal village where Tommy had a cousin. Their goal was a Swedish town called Landskrona, a walk of nearly ten and a half miles across the ice. They hoped the sea ice would hold. Worried about the possibility of weak ice, they would each carry a long pole to use to vault across fractures or small gaps—or to rescue each other. They'd also wear white under their overcoats, to avoid being spotted.

Late that night, they set off for the beach through the snow, trying to walk in only one set of footprints and avoid police lookout stations. On the shore, they tossed their dark overcoats to Tommy's cousin and tied themselves together for safety. They stepped onto the ice, now camouflaged against the white landscape. Tommy set the pace, urging Helvard to keep up. " 'You have to keep moving on ice because if you stand still you could go through.' "

It was silent, cold, and dark. They had a compass, their only guide in that long, harrowing night. After a while Tommy thought he made out on his left the outlines of Hven (now spelled Ven), a small Swedish island in the middle of the Øresund Sound. But it was hard to be sure. All they could do was to keep on toward their goal. At least the ice seemed firm enough to support them. Until dawn, that is.

That's when Tommy was startled by a sudden roar. " 'It was like rolling thunder and then we got scared, because two massive slabs of ice . . . just broke apart. If the fragmentation continued we knew the ice wouldn't be able to carry us. If the ice keeps breaking, finally you find yourself on such a small flake that you just go down with it, because it can't carry your weight. I knew how dangerous these conditions were from my childhood, walking on ice around Fanø. When I had fallen in as a boy I had been lucky to survive.' "

The wind picked up and snow swirled around them. They were close to the shipping lanes, where icebreakers routinely broke up ice to allow ships to pass. Now they could see a main fracture line racing toward them.

They'd have to retreat, back toward the island of Hven. As each second passed, their chances of being cut off from the main ice increased. They were about to be trapped unless they could vault over the break onto safer ice.

" 'When the biggest crack in the ice opened up, it blocked our path back to Hven. It was as wide as a bed is long, and I screamed at Arne to run at it and use his pole when I did. If you didn't have a run-up, you didn't have the momentum to get yourself lifted into the air, or the forward movement to land where you wanted to. It was a bit like pole-vaulting, but there was no real bend in the pole because it was made of wood. All the more reason why we really had to run at it.' "

Somehow they managed to land safely on the other side. They weren't out of danger yet though. It was now clear that getting across to Sweden was out of the question. The ice simply wouldn't support them. They weren't even sure they could outrun the rapidly disintegrating ice before they were sucked into the cold, deadly sea. To make matters worse, it was snowing heavier than ever, making it almost impossible to see.

All at once, Tommy picked out what looked like figures in the distance. Minutes later, men emerged out of the sleet and snow. They were Swedish policemen. " 'We thought they were our saviors but they treated us like criminals. . . . Still, at least they were dragging us onto solid ground, and that was good to know.' "

Tommy's harrowing physical ordeal had ended. But he wasn't out of danger yet.

A SPY'S END

Tommy Sneum had survived a daring flight across the North Sea, a dangerous parachute drop, and finally, a treacherous ice crossing. Now another fate hung over his head.

A Swedish policeman picked up Tommy and Arne Helvard on that March night of their escape, saying, "'I feel obliged to tell you . . . that they are going to send you to Germany, or at the very least back to the Germans in Denmark.'

"'I got scared when I heard that. . . . I knew that if the Germans got their hands on me, they would shoot me or torture me, or more likely both,'" Tommy said later.

Tommy hoped that, as the Princes had promised, someone was working on arrangements to get him to Great Britain. Since Sweden was neutral, officials there had to be careful not to anger the Germans by harboring suspected spies. Tommy was an unusual case. He seemed to have fallen through the cracks in Sweden, with no one to advocate for him, especially since the SIS was out of the picture and the SOE hadn't been told anything about him. The bold, brash Tommy was often angry during questioning, increasingly fearful that he had been completely abandoned by the British.

Eventually Tommy and his friend Arne Helvard were sent back to England. There they were put in Brixton Prison to undergo further interrogation. Even after Helvard was released, Tommy remained behind bars. There were some who thought

Christmas Møller.

he might be a double agent working for the Germans. He had to be cleared of all suspicion before he could be set free.

Finally, after several months, Tommy's situation came to the attention of Christmas Møller, a well-known Dane who had fled to Great Britain, where he played an influential role in broadcasting to Denmark for the BBC. Møller had a much better sense than Tommy of the internal politics among the SOE, the SIS, and the Princes of the Danish intelligence section. Møller visited Tommy in prison and, certain that Tommy was telling the truth about his actions, persuaded the SOE to look carefully at his case.

Thanks to Møller's persistence, Tommy was given a long hearing by two SOE officials, both of whom knew Denmark well. The usually hot-tempered Tommy spoke calmly, carefully describing the work he had done for the SIS, his escape to Sweden, and his fears that he would be turned over to the Germans.

Finally Tommy was cleared of suspicion. He had been held for more than six months. He was released around the beginning of October 1942. Since Møller had taken a strong interest in his fellow Dane, Tommy was given a job translating intelligence reports in his office.

But desk work didn't suit the action-loving Tommy. In late 1943, Tommy left London for Plymouth, England, where he became part of the Danish section of the British Royal Navy. Tommy knew he'd never be allowed to be a spy again. He had hoped that the British would take him on as a fighter pilot, but this was off-limits as well.

CHAPTER TWELVE

Officials told him he posed too great a risk. " 'They were worried that if I got shot down and survived someone might recognize me and then I would be tortured by the Germans and end up telling them everything I knew, which was plenty.' "

In May of 1944, a chance encounter led to an invitation for Tommy to join the Royal Norwegian Air Force. Tommy was assigned to defend the coast of Great Britain from attack. He would be flying again, although he wouldn't be involved in any direct combat missions.

At least Tommy was back in the skies, doing what he loved best.

CHAPTER THIRTEEN
UP FROM THE ASHES: THE SOE TRIES AGAIN

Tommy Sneum wasn't the only one who'd felt the ripples from the parachute accident that killed SOE chief organizer Carl Bruhn. In the spring of 1942, while Tommy was making his escape, Ralph Hollingworth sat in his London office struggling to cope with the death of a brilliant young man—and the failure of his first SOE operation.

Ralph's colleague Reginald Spink never forgot the day the telegram with the bad news arrived. "'There are some situations that become imprinted in one's memory like a fixed, never fading photographic negative. This was such an event—what had happened was the worst that could possibly happen. Bruhn had been killed in the jump.'"

What was next for the SOE? Radio operator Mogens Hammer hadn't been trained for the role of chief organizer and didn't possess Bruhn's leadership skills. Ralph would need to recruit a new leader.

Ralph was also busy changing other parts of his overall BOOKLET strategy for Denmark. The wartime landscape was shifting. Great Britain was no longer fighting Germany alone. After Hitler's invasion of the Soviet Union in June 1941, that country had turned against Germany and become a British ally. Then, following the Japanese attack on Pearl Harbor on December 7, 1941, the United States entered the war, adding American military might to the Allied effort. Fears that Great

Britain would be wiped out by the Germans lessened, although victory would still be years away.

Previously, the British had toyed with the idea of forming secret armies in the countries Germany occupied. Ralph had called this effort CHAIR in his overall plan. But after the United States entered the war, the idea of forming secret armies began to lose traction.

Instead, Great Britain and the United States turned their energies toward planning a combined invasion of Europe. Its code name was Operation Neptune. Today we know it as D-day. This massive Allied invasion of Normandy, on the French coast, would take a long time to plan and carry out (military planners began in 1942 and originally hoped to launch it in 1943; however, it didn't take place until June 6, 1944).

Although the SOE would no longer try to form a secret army in Denmark, building a network to conduct sabotage (TABLE) remained a top goal. Ralph found a Danish volunteer named Christian Michael Rottbøll to replace Carl Bruhn. The parachute operation to drop Rottbøll was given the code name Table Top. It was set for April 1942, just a few weeks after Tommy escaped to Sweden.

This time the SOE would send in a team of three: Rottbøll and two radio operators, Paul Johannesen and Max Johannes Mikkelsen. Their mission remained the same: to establish regular radio communications and build a network to collect information and conduct sabotage "against German shipping, against train ferries, and against supplies to and from Germany."

Christian Michael Rottbøll.

CHAPTER THIRTEEN

No one wanted a repeat of the situation in which Hammer had found himself—alone and without friends he could trust. This time, the men would have help waiting on the ground when they arrived. The SOE used contacts in Stockholm to alert a few trusted resistance workers in Denmark. The operation took place on the night of April 17, 1942. An activist named Eigil Borch-Johansen, code name the Duke, was tapped to pick up the men once they landed.

Borch-Johansen described what happened next: " 'The aircraft arrived according to plan, and the first landing went smoothly where it should. I ran out at once and met Rottbøll, and we exchanged code words, after which he set to work at once, packing the parachute and the rest of his things together, after I had shown him a small pond, where the whole lot could be submerged.'

" 'I then started looking for the others. I had heard the smack of the chutes, and had seen at least one container go down, although at some distance. During my search I heard the sound of footsteps, and now I found Johannesen, who had landed in a tree, and was hurt. He was a good deal shaken, and stood with his pistol cocked.' "

Despite hours of searching, they couldn't find the third parachutist, Mikkelsen. As it turned out, he too had landed in a tree but had fallen and been knocked out cold. When he awoke it was morning; the woods were deserted, and he was alone. Luckily Mikkelsen managed to get by train to Copenhagen on his own the next day.

•••

The work was dangerous. The SOE wanted to build a network throughout the country capable of conducting large-scale sabotage operations. That meant recruiting and training enough people willing to undertake great risk—not just in the actions themselves, but the possibility of being captured, tortured, and killed.

An effective, widespread sabotage effort couldn't be managed by individuals working alone, in the way rogue saboteur Niels Skov had been operating. To destroy a guarded factory that made parts for German vehicles required inside knowledge of the factory layout, enough explosives to do the job, and precise planning and coordination. It was far more complicated than setting fire to a single car.

As he faced this daunting challenge, Michael Rottbøll often felt frustrated with the slow pace of progress. Said Eigil Borch-Johansen, his fellow resistance worker: "'He was burning to get sabotage started. . . . He sometimes felt he was not accomplishing anything, but was wasting his time and his chances.'"

Establishing regular radio contact with Great Britain to share information was also a risky undertaking, even with more radio operators to help. Since the tragic accident with the parachute drop in Haslev a few months before, the Germans had become more alert than ever to illegal radio activity. They put pressure on the Danish police to locate the sites of illegal transmissions. It was critical to change the location often: The Germans had detection equipment that could locate the transmissions more easily if they were made from the same address.

CHAPTER THIRTEEN

Anyone whose apartment was being used for a radio transmission put themselves and their entire family in danger. Finding volunteers wasn't easy. People were "'very frightened of taking part in the work,'" radio operator Max Mikkelsen noted.

The SOE agents tried to take precautions. They cut transmission time and made an effort to change locations for each radio contact. Radio operator Duus Hansen reported that they'd also begun to post guards near the transmission point "'who could get in contact with the operator and warn him in case anything happened.'"

Unfortunately, sometimes radio transmissions were broadcast without an adequate warning system in place. That's what happened on September 5, 1942, a few months after the new agents arrived.

Radio operator Paul Johannesen had worked from the apartment of a friend on September 4. The next day, when he began transmitting again from the same spot, more than one hundred police officers stormed the apartment. The German counterespionage unit had directed the Danish police to search houses on a certain block; their direction finders had worked.

Johannesen had no time to flee. In the gunfire that followed, one police detective was killed. Knowing he would be tortured to reveal the names of fellow resistance fighters, Johannesen courageously swallowed a cyanide pill and died instantly.

The next week brought further crackdowns. A number of people working on an illegal newspaper were arrested. As for the fledgling SOE organization, one historian put it this way: "All its members were on the run."

Mogens Hammer, who'd been struggling to find his footing since Carl Bruhn had been killed, had become involved with that same illegal newspaper. If he were arrested, the consequences for the SOE would be severe. It was time for Hammer to get out, especially since Rottbøll was now able to take on the task of chief organizer. Borch-Johansen, "the Duke," who'd picked up Rottbøll and his team when they'd landed, was also in danger of arrest and would make the escape attempt along with Hammer.

But how to get to Sweden? It was September, a time of year without firm ice on the Sound. They decided to use a two-person kayak. Hammer and Borch-Johansen agreed to travel separately and meet near a friend's summer home on the coast before paddling to Sweden in a borrowed kayak.

As he hid in a thicket of raspberry bushes by the side of the road, Borch-Johansen imagined each car passing was the police and worried that Hammer had already been caught. " 'At last I heard footsteps on the road. They did not sound like Hammer's, and I saw the silhouette of a tall man, dressed in a long black overcoat, soft hat and carrying an umbrella,' " he recalled. " 'It was half a minute after he had passed by that I came out of my hiding place and found that it was Hammer, very well disguised as a kind of lay preacher. He had even managed to alter his walk.' "

They found their friend's summer house, along with the waiting kayak. A strong wind meant they had to wait another day before setting out. Finally it was time. " 'When darkness fell, we carried the boat down the slope, stuffed the luggage in and rowed out. We got well away from the coast, but soon had to row in again.' " Hammer, who was larger, had been sitting in the front rather than the rear, making steering too difficult.

They bailed out the kayak, changed places, and set off again. Before long they spied the lights of a patrol boat bearing down on them. They made for the beach to hide the kayak and themselves under some seaweed. Recalled Borch-Johansen: " 'We heard footsteps, and a man came towards us, carrying a fishing rod. We lay still in the dry seaweed, until the man came and poked us, and then we jumped up with pistols cocked, and drew his attention to the fact that it would be best for him if he did not inform anyone that he had seen us.' "

The fisherman told them German patrols often came to this spot. So even though it would soon be light, the two men set out again, paddling until they reached a more secluded, wooded section of the coast. Here, exhausted and soaked, they broke into a vacation cottage and slept through the day. Their luck held the next evening: The weather was fair. They ate their last raisins and chocolate and started out again just after midnight. By six the next morning they had landed safely in Sweden.

. . .

Meanwhile, with radio operator Paul Johannesen dead, SOE chief organizer Michael Rottbøll was left to pick up the pieces. He wanted to strengthen the warning system to protect the radio operators, and he also hoped to get more support from sympathetic Danish police on the inside. After all, the resistance and the police had a common enemy—the Nazis. Rottbøll worked to set up a secret understanding so that even if the Danish police felt pressured by the Germans to make arrests, no one on either side would open fire.

It was one of his last acts. Just weeks after Johannesen's death, two police officers were sent to locate Rottbøll. For whatever reason, they weren't aware of the agreement that Danes should not fire on one another. When the police knocked, Rottbøll answered the door in his pajamas, one hand behind his back. That hand held a gun.

Everything seemed to happen all at once. One policeman grabbed his arm. Rottbøll's gun went off. More shots followed. Rottbøll was hit by twelve bullets and died at the scene. The two policemen were not hurt.

Once again tragedy had struck. Nearly a year after Ralph Hollingworth had first launched TABLE, the effort to build sabotage groups in Denmark, the SOE still had no chief organizer.

●●●

After his escape, Mogens Hammer didn't expect to return to Denmark during the war. He had done the best he could ever since the night when, after Carl Bruhn's death, he'd been forced to step into the role of the SOE's chief organizer. Hammer didn't learn of Michael Rottbøll's death until he arrived safely in London at the end of September 1942. Almost immediately, Ralph Hollingworth came to see him. He had an unexpected appeal.

Said Ralph: " 'I asked him to go back at once and carry on

the work, and in spite of his astonishment at my request, and his strong impression that in the circumstances he would be in a very difficult position, he accepted, which shows what a brave man he was. . . . I calculated that the Germans, once he had left the country, would think that the last thing he would do would be to come back, and come back at once.' "

Ralph felt he had no choice. He had no one else ready or willing to coordinate the treacherous, frustrating work of creating an organized resistance network inside an occupied country. Like Tommy Sneum, Hammer was willing to do whatever it took. His tasks over the next few months in Denmark would be simply to keep the network together and prepare for the next SOE chief organizer—all while not getting caught by the Nazis. Hammer managed to slip back secretly into the country via parachute.

The last year had been a difficult one for the SOE. Two chief organizers and one radio operator had already been killed. Even with courageous men like Mogens Hammer, it was clear things weren't going well. But that was about to change.

SPRING 1943: FIRE STARTER

Like Tommy Sneum, Niels Skov was all about action and taking matters into his own hands. He'd begun his secret sabotage operations in the first months after the occupation, and nearly two years on, he hadn't stopped. News from the outside world on the progress of the war was encouraging. There was a feeling that the tide might be turning. That fueled his impatience, making him bolder.

In March 1943, while in his hometown of Ribe visiting family, Niels set his sights on a new sabotage target. His old friend Aage Kjellerup no longer lived there, so Niels was on his own. When he walked by the Ford auto repair shop and saw German vehicles being serviced, it seemed an opportunity too good to resist. Late one evening, he snuck in through a missing windowpane, picking his way among the military vehicles. He tried to memorize the layout.

He returned the next night. "With my eyes adjusted to the dark, I started methodically to carry out my plan. First, I piled a dozen tires into a weapons carrier that was blocking the main exit and proceeded to drench them with kerosene."

Next he let out oil from two storage barrels and punctured the gas tank of a motorcycle. Matches were still his main sabotage material. First, Niels lit wood shavings around the side of the building. "Matches in hand, I raced to the entrance door to the shop and threw a lighted match through the glassless window onto the gasoline trail inside. With the gasping sound of a giant boxer being hit in the stomach, the room belched into instant flame."

Racing into the darkness, Niels headed for his grandparents' house and was soon in bed. A little while later, when the fire department horns woke the neighborhood, Niels joined the curious crowd of onlookers watching the building be devoured by flames.

A man Niels had known all his life turned to the crowd and said, " 'Well . . . one thing I can tell you. This fire was set by English agents. Danes don't do this sort of thing.' "

Niels turned away and went home to bed. The man was wrong. Some Danes were doing this sort of thing—and in time they would do a lot more of it.

■ ■ ■

Even without the organized network Ralph Hollingworth and the SOE envisioned, the number of sabotage incidents in Denmark was beginning to increase. An underground group known as BOPA, affiliated with the Danish Communist Party (DKP), had been active since 1942 and would continue to be a major player in sabotage actions throughout the war. BOPA (an abbreviation of the Danish for *bourgeois partisans*, or middle-class partisans) eventually attracted a diverse group of members including carpenters, doctors, students, metal workers, auto mechanics, artists, and many others. BOPA and another group called Holger Danske, named after a legendary Danish folk hero, would become the country's two largest sabotage organizations.

Sometimes, especially in the early years of the occupation,

sabotage was undertaken by individuals like Niels Skov or by small, informal groups. One of the most well known was formed by two brothers, Knud and Jens Pedersen. In honor of Winston Churchill, they called it the Churchill Club. The group was made up of eleven teenage boys who carried out more than two dozen actions, including burning a freight train carrying military supplies. Its young members were arrested and jailed in May 1942.

The Danish government continued to try to discourage sabotage activities. On September 2, 1942, the Danish prime minister broadcast a radio speech calling for law and order, denouncing the expansion of illegal publications and acts of sabotage. He warned Danish citizens that the increase in sabotage could have serious repercussions: The Nazis would crack down if Denmark's cooperation agreement with

Four SOE operatives who were photographed after the war, including Knud Pedersen, founder of the Churchill Club, on the far left.

CHAPTER FOURTEEN

Germany changed. Danish citizens arrested for sabotage would face the death penalty, and the Danish government wouldn't be able to help them.

The prime minister also made clear that the government and police couldn't combat sabotage alone. He encouraged informers and called for citizens to help: " 'This requires the cooperation of all the good powers in our people, of all who have insight and influence over others, and those who are entrusted with leadership.' "

Yet while many Danes still supported accommodating the Germans, feelings of resentment and frustration about the German occupation continued to smolder. Just a few days after the prime minister spoke, Christmas Møller used his BBC broadcast from London to encourage all Danes to embrace sabotage.

" 'Action is required of us all, of each one of us. . . . The outcome of this gigantic struggle concerns us all. . . . It is our duty to have only one thing in view, that which hurts Germany most and that which benefits the cause of our Allies. . . . Damage and delays, bombing and Resistance action—these are the means by which, with increasing effect, we will suffocate and strangle the German transport organization. Do your duty—do your work.' "

While most Danes were still unwilling to accept sabotage as a legitimate means of protest, by the spring of 1943, the situation was beginning to change. Within a year, the flames of resistance, fanned by news of German battle defeats, calls for sabotage from the illegal press, and the actions of small groups of activists, would soon be unstoppable.

Along the way, what would eventually become a blazing momentum for change began to draw in more people who'd been on the sidelines, not quite ready to commit themselves to action. Medical student Jørgen Kieler was one of them.

SPRING 1943: THE FLAMES BEGIN TO TAKE HOLD

Since the day the Nazis arrived, Jørgen Kieler and his friends had been debating how best to fight the German invasion. For a long time, Jørgen hadn't felt ready to become a saboteur or spy. "I had no idea about sabotage techniques, knew nothing about weapons, or about objects to be targeted," he reflected.

Yet whenever other students gathered in the apartment he and his siblings shared, the talk always came back to the occupation. What could they do against the Nazis? How could the actions of a few individuals change things? As the months progressed, the students felt that just talking wasn't enough. It was, Jørgen reflected, like living under "daily moral pressure, and a solution had to be found."

On occasion, Jørgen had delivered copies of underground newssheets. Even this activity carried risks. Just a few months before, in September of 1942, the Germans had used a sympathetic Danish informant to infiltrate an illegal publication, *De Frie Danske* (*The Free Danes*), and subsequently imprison four people. Following that roundup, another thirty people were arrested.

Then, in December, some prominent leaders of the underground publication *Frit Danmark (Free Denmark)*, including the influential doctor and professor of surgery Ole Chievitz (the man who'd helped Tommy Sneum after he was hurt in his parachute drop), had been arrested.

An assortment of illegal newspapers printed in Denmark during World War II.

CHAPTER FIFTEEN

Although he'd been warned in advance by a sympathetic Danish police officer, Chievitz had made a bold decision: He would not try to evade arrest. Instead, he hoped that the action against a well-known community leader like himself "'would attract attention and make people think.'" It did just that, and supporters circulated petitions calling for his release.

Another professor who'd been involved with *Frit Danmark*, Mogens Fog, went into hiding and penned an open letter calling for action: "'Do not think we can avoid the nightmare under Nazi tyranny by being compliant. There is only one way, the primitive way—to resist.'" (Fog would go on in September of 1943 to help form an executive committee aimed at coordinating the work of all active resistance groups. Called the Freedom Council, it brought together representatives from the illegal press, academics, religious organizations, and others; the SOE chief organizer participated as an outside observer.)

At the end of December 1942, Jørgen had been approached by a fellow medical student and asked to pass out copies of Fog's letter to other students and friends. Jørgen read it "with great emotion and excitement. . . . Fog called upon us all to take . . . personal responsibility for the outcome of the war. And to those who were uncertain as to the use of Danish resistance, he wrote, 'Only a drop in the ocean, that's what they say. Well now, the ocean consists of drops.'"

The student who'd given Jørgen the letter had another request too: There was a need for a new location to help produce copies of *Frit Danmark*. Could the group use the Kielers' apartment? Despite the danger, Jørgen and his brother and

Mogens Fog.

sisters didn't hesitate to say yes. "We could wait no longer. . . . Two and a half years of wandering in the wilderness were over."

And so, in early 1943, when they returned to Copenhagen after the holidays, the Kieler siblings and a few friends began meeting to help produce the illegal newssheet, becoming part of the Free Denmark Student Group. The articles them- selves were written by an anonymous editorial committee. Like other groups in place throughout the country, the Kielers would type up the pieces and produce copies of the illegal newssheets on a small duplicating machine to distribute to fellow students and ordinary citizens. While the machine was moved from place to place for safety's sake, the Kielers' apart- ment became the group's central meeting place.

Jørgen and his friends took to the work with enthusiasm, "banging away on an old typewriter, making stencils, using masses of ink and a good duplicator." They used old manual typewriters, and since no one could touch-type, everyone "typed away with one finger."

It was a hands-on, time-consuming process. These were the days before computers and laser printers. Copies were made by typing stencils, which were then run through a duplicating machine. Each stencil could make about two hundred sheets before wearing out. Later they got an electric duplicator that could make five hundred copies from each stencil.

"We would write until late into the night and would despair if a stencil fell to pieces when it was nearly ready. This had to be repaired with nail varnish, or be rewritten; the newssheet *had* to be published," Jørgen recalled.

Jørgen and the other students working for *Frit Danmark*

were part of a growing illegal press movement that had begun shortly after the invasion. In March of 1943, about 80 different underground newspapers were being published; two years later that number had grown to 265, with more than 2.5 million copies of illegal papers being distributed each month. An underground (and, again, illegal) news agency maintained connections with papers in the free world outside Denmark to keep communication and news flowing. The British Broadcasting Corporation (BBC), with regular broadcasts in Danish by Christmas Møller in London, was also a part of this expanding communication effort.

■ ■ ■

Meanwhile, as Jørgen Kieler typed fiery words of protest in *Frit Danmark* and Niels Skov scouted for sabotage targets to set on fire, the SOE made yet another attempt to put a leader on the ground to help with that very work. Maybe this time conditions would be right.

The SOE's new leader, Flemming Muus, parachuted into the country secretly on March 11, 1943. Called by Ralph Hollingworth "'a born organizer,'" Muus was charged with building on the work Mogens Hammer and Michael Rottbøll had begun. (With a new SOE chief organizer in place, Hammer, who'd been trying to build a network of volunteers as best he could, was able to escape Denmark once again, leaving that spring. Unfortunately Hammer was killed in a ship accident in early 1946.)

Muus seemed perfect for the job and went to work with a passion. He became known for his disciplined approach and

An illegal newspaper published in Horsens, Denmark—Jørgen Kieler's hometown.

insistence on tight security. Under his leadership, an effective resistance effort began to take shape. For the first time, Great Britain could make regular airdrops of sabotage material to local SOE groups. Muus also made contact with the Princes of the Danish intelligence staff, using his diplomatic skills to work toward more cooperation between officials in Great Britain and Denmark. And he was in contact with other Danish resistance groups through the Freedom Council. At last, the SOE had a chief organizer who could make things happen—and stay alive.

Sabotage began to have an impact. Between March and September 1943, nineteen flights from Great Britain dropped seventy-nine cartons containing explosives, detonators, and ammunition for use by Danish saboteurs. That number increased dramatically in the final two years of the war; in 1945, more than four thousand containers carrying 439 tons of material were dropped to aid sabotage efforts.

The SOE's Ralph Hollingworth and Ronald Turnbull had waited a long time for success. Turnbull wrote to his friend and colleague: " 'We seem to have been piling rocks and stone and concrete into the swamp in order to make a solid foundation for our railway. Often it has seemed as if the foundation was strongly laid, but then quite suddenly a soft patch has occurred, and we have had to start piling more rock into the swamp. . . . Throughout these two years I have always felt sure that sooner or later your efforts and, to a small degree mine, would be rewarded. Now at any rate it looks as if at last we have a solid foundation and are now able to lay the lines confidently.' "

SPRING 1943: THE FLAMES BEGIN TO TAKE HOLD

Muus continued as the SOE's chief organizer until December 1944, when he was pulled out to escape an intense hunt by Gestapo agents. He was replaced in February 1945 by Ole Lippman, the SOE's last chief organizer in Denmark, who was active until the end of the war, in May 1945.

■ ■ ■

By April 1943, the illegal publication *Frit Danmark* reported that " 'the call to sabotage has caught on among the population. From week to week, more and more Danish enterprises which work for the Germans are reported wrecked. . . . More sabotage, more blockage of deliveries of war material, more unreliable products will no doubt mean unpleasantness for the country for the moment—but it shortens the war and opens the way to our freedom in the future.' "

Jørgen Kieler began to feel at odds with himself. Was it enough to simply be involved in the illegal press? His sisters, Elsebet and Bente, were against violence. Jørgen wasn't sure where he stood. But he had to ask himself a hard question: "Could I be encouraging others to become saboteurs if I myself were not prepared to run the risk involved?"

Then Jørgen learned that a captured Danish saboteur had been sentenced to death by the Germans. The news brought matters to a head for him. "Denmark's ever-increasing contribution to the German war machine, which took on the form of food, industrial products, repair work and transport, were all helping to sustain a criminal war.

"This . . . had to be stopped. . . . And so I made my decision."

The time to act had come.

Frit Danmark

. Aarg. Nr. 5   Udgivet af en Kreds af Danske   August 19

Begivenhederne nærmer sig Danmark
Nu maa Rigsdagen handle

Saafremt den danske Rigsdag vil røgte et Hverv, Folket for blot nogle Maaneder siden tillidsfuldt lagde i dens Hænder, aa maa den nu, *netop nu*, offentligt, *netop ffentligt*, give tilkende, at den efter de idste Dages militære og storpolitiske Beivenheder er sig sit Ansvar bevidst.

Hvad Churchill, Roosevelt og Eisenower har sagt til Italienerne, gælder for s som for alle af tysk Nazisme voldførte olk: *de maa stege i deres eget Fedt*, og e maa lide Savn, Nød og Ydmygelse, og e maa finde sig i de Allieredes Land-, ø- og Luftvaabens Hærgen, indtil de selv iger sig fri af direkte og indirekte Samrbejde med Hitler og hans korrupte Bander. Vover den danske Rigsdag at idde disse Advarsler overhørig?

Uligheden mellem de Tilstande, som ersker i Danmark og i de egentlig krigsørende Lande, hvad enten de som Runænien, Ungarn, Italien og Finland er Iitlers Forbundsfæller, eller de — som rankrig — lever under en Slags Vaabentilstands Kaar, eller de endelig er hans nidlertidigt slagne Fjender som Norge, Belgien, Holland, Jugoslavien og Grækenand — — disse Uligheder er saa iøjnealdende, at den ved ubehagelige Samnenligninger sædvanlig anvendte Replik: Det er noget helt andet«, denne Gang kke kan faa Betydning for andre end nalfabeter.

Det Spørgsmaal, som foreligger, skal kke besvares ved Paavisning af Uligeder mellem Danmarks og f. Eks. Itaiens Forhold til Hitler-Tyskland, men ed *Erkendelse af de Ligheder*, som efter le allierede Stormagters paa givne Kendserninger støttede Opfattelse vitterlig finres mellem Danmark og andre Lande, r tiener den tyske Krigsmaskine og rved unyttigt forlænger Krigen og selv

paatager sig den dermed forbund uhyre Risiko.

Eller er det ikke en for Verden aabe bar Kendsgerning, at Danmark territo alt, økonomisk og finansielt lader sig nytte af Hitler-Tyskland i Krigen m de allierede Nationer?

Jo, det *er* en for Verden aabenb Kendsgerning, at saadan, *netop saa* spiller Danmark sin Rolle i Tidens D ma — og har spillet den uafbrudt si 9. April 1940.

Vist saa, vil Indvendingerne lyde, saa, men under Protest og under O magts Tvang.

Lad gaa med Protesten. Den foreli — vil vi da haabe — forsvarligt do menteret.

Men *Tvangen?* Lader ogsaa den si kumentere, vel at mærke saaledes, dens Anvendelse ikke blot overbevi os selv, men — hvad der i den givne tuation er afgørende — de allierede St magter?

Det er ikke tilstrækkeligt at forta om Trusler. Naturligvis har Tyske ruttet med Trusler. Truslen er den fej Hovedvaaben. Spørgsmaalet er de *netop dette*, om den Scavenianske Re ring har bøjet sig allerede for Trusler eller om den i store og smaa Anliggen har ventet at give efter for O magtens *Tvang?*

Man kan ogsaa simplificere ved stille Spørgsmaalet saaledes, om det med den tyske Kniv paa Struben, Erik Scavenius paa det danske Fo Vegne udtalte sin beundrende Forb selse over Hitler-Tysklands Sejre, sk under paa Antikomintern-Pagten, b med Sovjetunionen og Kina, udlever xore Torpedobaade, desarmerede to diedele af vor Hær, lod os plyndre

The front page of the August 1943 issue of Frit Danmark.

AUGUST 1943:
A FATEFUL SUNDAY

Jørgen Kieler had crossed a bridge. He was no longer simply a concerned college student. By the summer of 1943, he was ready to put his life on the line.

"Once I had decided to take part in sabotage, I cycled home to Horsens . . . in order to make contact with a younger former schoolmate, Peer Borup," he wrote. "We were by now completely involved in the struggle against the Germans and their Danish collaborators. . . . All that was lacking in Horsens was sabotage."

They settled on a railway bridge for their first sabotage attempt. Jørgen knew they faced challenges. "The first was a lack of explosives; the second was the total lack of knowledge as to how to go about blowing up a railway bridge and the third was an imperfect idea of how long it would take to repair the bridge."

Borup contacted a shoemaker he knew who was also involved in the resistance. The man was able to provide some explosives and provide basic instructions on how to use them. They had to set the bombs by cycling to the bridge in the rain. Jørgen said, "We cycled very carefully out for the fear that the bomb could explode at the slightest jolt."

Once at the bridge, the two friends attached the explosive devices between two girders and pedaled home as fast as they could. The shoemaker had told Borup that the fuse could be lit an hour before the explosion, giving them enough time

A Danish saboteur sets an explosive along a railroad track in 1944.

CHAPTER SIXTEEN

to make their getaway and be safely in bed before the explosion.

"I went to bed immediately, but could not get to sleep," said Jørgen. "I was listening anxiously for the explosion and worrying about all those windows that would be shattered. . . . I think that I did hear an explosion—but a very small one, so I was not sure. Then I fell asleep."

The next morning, Jørgen and Borup rose early and cycled back to the bridge. Jørgen was relieved that no windows in nearby houses had been damaged. He was disappointed to see, though, that the bridge was intact: They had failed in their attempt to disrupt shipments of war materials to Germany. The only damage was a ten-inch hole and a few missing nails. As it turned out, one of the bombs they set hadn't even gone off.

Jørgen and Borup decided to learn from their mistake and try again. "We had started from scratch without any contact with the SOE, without any . . . instructions coming from Britain, without any knowledge of explosives, nor any assistance from any experts. . . . What we would now have to do is establish contact with someone who knew what sabotage was all about, because we certainly did not."

Jørgen headed back to his apartment in the city that afternoon, determined not to give up. That's when he first heard what had happened in Copenhagen while he'd been standing on the bridge that morning.

The date was Sunday, August 29, 1943. Once more, everything in Denmark had changed overnight.

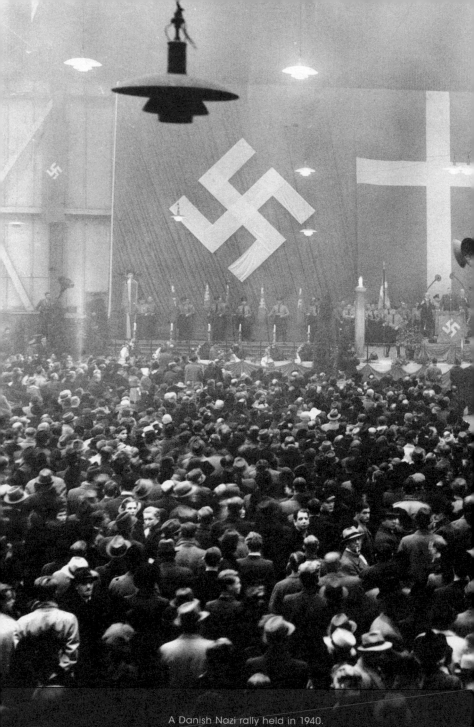

A Danish Nazi rally held in 1940.

PART TWO

CRACKDOWN & FLIGHT

SUMMER–FALL 1943

Courage is never alone, for it has fear as its
ever-present companion.

—Shlomo Breznitz

Two of my friends have disappeared, so the
rest of us are pretty worried.

—Kim Malthe-Bruun, December 3, 1944

martial law (n): military government, involving
the suspension of ordinary law.

plenipotentiary (n): a person, especially a
diplomat, invested with the full power of
independent action on behalf of his or her
government, typically in a foreign country.

rescue (v): to save (someone) from a dangerous or difficult situation.

CHAPTER SEVENTEEN
DENMARK SAYS NO

> It was Sunday, and a strange silence had
> settled over the land.
>
> —Jørgen Kieler

The man who headed the German occupation in Denmark was Dr. Werner W. Best, who'd been in the position of high plenipotentiary since November 1942. He prided himself on keeping Denmark stable, ensuring that supplies and foodstuffs were reaching Germany, and, all in all, being the right man for the job.

Best had continued to assure Hitler and his top lieutenants that he had everything under control in Denmark. He'd made a glowing report to his superiors in Berlin just that spring, pointing to the positive aspects of the situation: The Danes were continuing to send food and factory goods to Germany; the country was peaceful; everything was running well. And if there were more sabotage incidents than previously, well, these could be blamed on Great Britain and the parachutists they'd dropped. Best had concluded that Denmark was a "'country without major problems.'" The reason for success? The answer was obvious: his own abilities to manage a complicated and delicate situation.

Yet by the summer of 1943, anyone could see that things were starting to get out of hand. On July 6 of that year, more than a hundred Danish civilians were arrested in Copenhagen after a confrontation with Germans and an aggressive group

CHAPTER SEVENTEEN

of Nazi sympathizers, as well as Danes who had become volunteer soldiers fighting for Germany in a Danish Nazi organization called Frikorps Danmark. Frikorps Danmark had been formed by the feared and powerful Heinrich Himmler, the Nazi leader who headed a group within the Nazi party called the SS (Schutzstaffel) and who was responsible for setting up and controlling the concentration camps that killed millions. The Danish volunteers recruited for Frikorps Danmark took part in military training and were indoctrinated with extreme Nazi ideas.

The Copenhagen incident was sparked, in part, when two Frikorps soldiers knocked a young woman wearing a cap with a British Royal Air Force (RAF) emblem off her bicycle. Tensions ran high, and the afternoon turned violent, with Frikorps soldiers attacking civilians. Undeterred, young Danes continued to wear the RAF caps throughout the summer. The caps became a symbol of protest against a future where Denmark would be part of a larger Nazi empire.

Danish civilians were also encouraged by news of Allied military victories elsewhere. Germany was experiencing losses at sea; in May the Nazis had surrendered in North Africa, and Allied forces had invaded Italy in late June. For Danes suffering since 1940 under German occupation, the changing tides of war gave people more confidence to resist. Unlike the early days of the conflict, when Germany seemed unstoppable, there was now a sense that Denmark might be able to rise up against the invaders and drive them out.

For Werner Best, charged with overseeing Denmark for the Germans, things went from bad to worse in late July and

A German SS officer stops a girl wearing a hat with the RAF symbol.

August of 1943. Workers at the Odense Steel Shipyard were being forced to build a German mine-laying ship. On July 28, after a saboteur blew a hole in the ship's hull, the Germans posted armed guards at the shipyard. In protest, Danish employees staged a sit-down strike, and workers in other places in the city followed suit. This grassroots action led to success; armed German guards were removed from several Odense businesses.

News of this victory led to protests elsewhere. Then, back in Odense, tensions ignited again. Citizens overturned Danish police vehicles; Germans patrolled the streets in large trucks, sometimes shooting randomly. In response, Danes broke windows and burned furniture of those known to be collaborating with the Nazis. German and Danish reinforcements arrived. One historian described Odense as " 'a city in open revolt.' "

Volunteers from Denmark who enlisted to fight for the Germans on the Eastern front march to their barracks under the flag of the Frikorps Danmark.

Like a forest fire, the flames of defiance jumped from place to place. In Aalborg, a young man was killed and ten thousand people marched to the graveyard for his funeral, hurling stones at German soldiers. As clashes between crowds and German soldiers escalated, more people were wounded; some were killed. The Danish government called on its citizens to preserve the peace. But the time for peaceful submission to the German occupation was coming to a close.

On August 24, in the midst of what came to be called the August Rebellion, Werner Best was summoned to German headquarters in Berlin to answer for what was happening on his watch. He was told it was time to crack down and was given a list of demands to pass on to the Danish government, which would simply have to do more to control its citizens and restrain protests. The demands included a curfew across the nation, special courts to sentence rioters, and imposing the death penalty for anyone caught doing sabotage.

At 9:00 a.m. on Saturday, August 28, 1943, Best presented Danish officials with the list of demands. It was a pivotal moment—the showdown activists had been hoping would take place. The ultimatum had a deadline: An answer was required by 4:00 p.m. that day. The conditions were final. Take it or leave it; no negotiation would be allowed.

Up to this point, the Danish government had collaborated with the Nazis in large part to keep the peace and protect its people. Now the balancing act that had kept Denmark "normal" had frayed beyond repair.

The government could not agree to—or enforce—these new measures, which included putting its own citizens to

Werner Best.

death for protesting the occupation. For instance, one un-acceptable condition stipulated that "Danish police officers would hunt down militant members of the Resistance, and that these members would be condemned to death under Danish law and executed by their own compatriots."

Just before the deadline, at 3:45 p.m., the Danish government gave its answer: a resounding no. The statement said, in part, that the government "regrets that it cannot find it right to help in carrying through" the demands being made to crack down on citizens.

At 4:00 a.m. the next day, Sunday, August 29, 1943, the Germans imposed a state of emergency in Denmark. Germans attacked the Copenhagen naval base. Ship commanders had their instructions: to surrender under protest, which meant blowing up their own vessels and sinking them before the Germans could mount an attack.

"By the morning of August 29, when the inhabitants of Copenhagen awoke, the Danish Army and Navy had been neutralized, German soldiers were standing guard at all buildings of importance, telephones no longer rang, and mail service had been cut off. . . . Martial law had come to Denmark," wrote one historian.

As he arrived back in Copenhagen from his hometown that day, Jørgen Kieler caught sight of a proclamation announcing the crackdown and some of the new rules. There could be no gatherings of more than five people. Cars and trucks had to be off the road at sundown. Strikes were forbidden; trying to organize a strike that damaged Germany

A train derailed by an act of sabotage in 1943.

Nordbjærg & Wedell's Boat Yard in Copenhagen burns after sabotage in April 1943.

would be punished by death. Any acts of violence or worker strikes would be ruthlessly suppressed by force of arms.

■ ■ ■

No one knew what would happen next, or what military rule would mean. But Jørgen and other activists shared the same reaction: This was a victory for the Danish people. Sabotage, strikes, and acts of resistance had brought Denmark to a breaking point.

Jørgen put it this way: "AT LAST—Denmark had finally said NO."

CHAPTER EIGHTEEN
THE WARNING

> Where there is room in the heart, there is room in the house.
>
> —Danish proverb

Since that terrifying April morning three years before, when enemy planes had filled the skies, the Danish government had stood between ordinary citizens and the occupying German army. Now Germany was in total control. This change brought with it fears that the Nazis would act against Danish Jews, just as they had done elsewhere in Europe.

The Germans hadn't made any move to persecute Jews in Denmark since the occupation began in 1940, in part because the Danish government had made it clear the country wouldn't welcome anti-Jewish restrictions or laws. That meant most Jewish people had continued to hold jobs, go to school, and practice their religion. (Some prominent Jews in Denmark had been removed from their positions, and others had withdrawn from public life to avoid attracting attention from the Nazis, however.)

What would this new state of emergency mean to the Jewish people of Denmark, who up until now had escaped persecution? It wouldn't take long to find out.

• • •

At first glance, Georg Duckwitz seems an unlikely hero in the story of Denmark during World War II. He was, after all, a

Georg Ferdinand Duckwitz.

German who worked as an attaché under Werner Best in Copenhagen. Yet Duckwitz had close Danish friends and had lived in Denmark before the war broke out. Duckwitz drew his own line in the sand as to how far he would go to support his country, and what lines of decent human behavior he would not cross.

After the crackdown and the Nazi imposition of military rule in late August 1943, Duckwitz was put to the test. He first learned from Best on September 18 that a roundup of Danish Jews would soon take place. The next night he wrote in his diary, " 'I know what I have to do.' "

In the days that followed, Duckwitz tried to protest the action in Berlin; he also made a trip to Sweden to arrange for help for Jewish refugees there. Then, on Tuesday, September 28, he learned that the deportation of Danish Jews would begin in just a few days—on Friday night, October 1. The Germans planned to send ships to the port of Copenhagen and round up thousands of men, women, and children in the course of a single night.

Duckwitz met secretly with some of his Danish contacts. His warning mobilized others to spread the word throughout the Jewish community. There were 7,700 Jews in Denmark. People would have to act quickly.

■ ■ ■

The next day, Wednesday, September 29, sixteen-year-old Herbert Pundik was sitting in French class in his school in Copenhagen when the headmaster appeared in the door-way. He summoned Herbert and a couple of other boys into the hall, adding, " 'If there are any others among you of Jewish descent, you had better come along.' " At that, Herbert's teacher packed his books and left the room too.

" 'We have been warned that persecution of the Jews will soon begin,' the headmaster told Herbert and the others. 'You had better hurry home. The Germans may be here at any moment.' "

Herbert ran back to his desk, packed his schoolbag, and left the class in silence. "We knew that, at best, it might be a long time before we would see each other again. The boy who shared my desk had just time to hand me his boy-scout compass as a going-away present before I rushed out again."

At home, Herbert's parents and brothers were waiting, already dressed in warm clothing. Herbert's father had been warned that morning by a friend who'd passed on his rabbi's instructions: No Jewish family should spend the night at home.

Looking back, Herbert was struck by just how much he and his family did not know. They didn't know that millions of Jews had already been killed by the Germans, or what would happen to Denmark in the future. "We hardly knew where we would be spending the next night. We had no idea how we would manage to escape across The Sound to Sweden. Who would help us get in touch with the fishermen along the coast or the members of the resistance movement?"

Herbert was sure of only this: "From one hour to the next we had become homeless."

All he had to his name now was a bag with a few clothes in it. His stamp collection, favorite books, and postcard collection had to be left behind.

"We were frightened, lost and alone."

• • •

Herbert Pundik later discovered that several of his Christian friends and neighbors had been part of the effort to warn Jewish families like his own. One was seventeen-year-old Robert Pedersen, who would go on to a career as a member of parliament in later years. After Pedersen's father had heard the news from friends, he sent his son out to warn their entire neighborhood.

"'I went from house to house. . . . Whenever I saw a name plate that indicated a Jewish family, I rang the doorbell and asked to talk to them,'" Pedersen said. "'Sometimes they did not believe me. But I succeeded in persuading them to pack and come with me to Bispebjerg Hospital which had been turned into a gathering place for Jewish refugees.'"

Pedersen's first stop had been to a classmate, David Sompolinsky, and his family. "'There was light on the third floor where they lived. I knocked hard on the door. David opened it. I asked to talk to his father, but he said that they were celebrating his sister's wedding and did not wish to be disturbed. I said that what I wanted to discuss with his father was a matter of life and death.'"

David and his parents could barely absorb the enormity of the news. "'We kept on not wanting to believe it. After all, this

The German Gestapo rounding up Danish Jews in Copenhagen in October 1943.

was a country in which I had grown up, where I had no quarrel with anyone at all. I had had no contact of any kind with the German soldiers. It seemed unreasonable to assume that they, without warning, without any moral right, would arrest and deport citizens of the country,'" David recalled. "'We could not get used to the thought that it might happen here. . . . Was it conceivable that at the issue of an order they could turn overnight into the worst of predators?'"

Family members began to debate whether this was just another rumor. But in the end everyone was finally convinced by Pedersen's urgent pleas. Said David: "'In a half-choked voice he asked us to leave the house. . . . He repeatedly begged us to believe him and left the house with tears in his eyes.'"

■ ■ ■

The roundup of Danish Jews began on Friday evening, October 1, 1943. In readiness, the Germans had stationed two ships in Copenhagen Harbor and had a train with forty cattle cars standing by to transport people. Fifty flatbed trucks and German police cars were sent out through the streets of Copenhagen that night. The Germans had already gathered the names and addresses of Jewish families in Denmark.

A resistance activist named Erling Foss reported: "'Police vans proceeded to take up their position at certain spots, from where the arresting columns were sent out. At the same time the telephone services were completely suspended. . . . The roundup was carried out in various ways—it is difficult to get a clear picture. Some patrols were content merely to ring and to go away again if the door was not opened. Elsewhere,

CHAPTER EIGHTEEN

and this occurred often, they smashed in the door and woke up the whole house to cross-examine people in the other apartments as to the whereabouts of the Jews.'"

Arrests that night in Copenhagen numbered about two hundred, which included elderly residents of a Jewish nursing home, with another eighty-two Jews captured elsewhere. Yet something remarkable had taken place—most of the apartments the German police visited were empty. Almost all the Jews had been warned and gone into hiding by the time the police patrols arrived. Some families stayed with friends and business acquaintances; others went to hospitals, where Danish administrators, doctors, and nurses found ways to hide them until escape arrangements could be made.

While thousands of Jewish families had gone underground, it would take time to get them safely out of the country. Like other areas of the resistance movement, ordinary people stepped up to make that happen. Niels Skov, who'd taken action from almost the beginning of the occupation, was one of them. And, as usual, he went about it in his own creative way.

CHAPTER NINETEEN
UNDER NAZI NOSES

Ever since the moment when he had first decided to defy the Germans with nothing more than a screwdriver and a match, Niels Skov had avoided getting involved with a large group. He had acted alone or sometimes teamed up with a friend or small group of like-minded friends.

But Niels had expanded his efforts. In addition to sabotage, he'd begun helping with one of the underground newspapers, called *Hjemmefronten (The Home Front)*. Through this work, Niels met another activist, named Carlo Marqvard Thomsen, who went by the cover name of Poul Thiessen. Niels knew him simply as Thies.

Thies was ideally suited to work on producing an underground newsletter. Niels recalled, "A printing press mechanic by trade, he was an exceptionally fine craftsman and had intimate knowledge of just about every printing press in Copenhagen."

Thies was also cool under pressure and liked to make jokes. The two made a good team, though often Niels couldn't stop himself from laughing at something Thies said— even when they found themselves in a tight spot. Thies, Niels decided, "would stick to me like a brother." The two friends worked on printing the newssheets as well as sabotage activities, managing to stay "one short jump ahead of the Germans."

...

CHAPTER NINETEEN

Two nights after the failed roundup of Danish Jews, Niels and Thies met for a beer at a bistro near Copenhagen Harbor to discuss how they could help. They knew many Jewish families were still in hiding, trying to find a way out of Copenhagen to be transported across to Sweden from small villages along the coast.

Suddenly Thies looked at Niels. "'The easiest, of course, would be to gather them here and ship them out from Lynettehavnen.'"

The idea made sense. Although part of Copenhagen's large harbor complex, the docks of Lynettehavnen were somewhat out of the way, offering the chance of a bold escape plan right in plain sight. Niels weighed the suggestion: It had a lot of appeal—but also risk.

On the one hand, Niels figured, "The place could be quickly reached from the city's thousand hiding places, far better than transporting people up the coast toward Elsinore and exposing them in less populated surroundings. But I was also aware that the Germans were at top alert, probably trying to make up for their recent lack of success."

He knew of at least one fisherman who might be willing to help. The most dangerous part would be finding a way to get people to the harbor itself. As the two friends sat looking out, Thies suddenly had the answer. "'You know, if we could grab one of the canal boats that would be the perfect transport . . . to Lynettehavnen, directly to the fishing boat.'"

From his seat at the window, Niels looked out at a stop for one of the city's canal boats, which connected to the harbor and served as "watery avenues." Why, if they put out the word,

A fishing boat carrying Jews out of Denmark to safety in Sweden in October 1943. This photograph was taken by one of the refugees.

perhaps they could even collect people right in front of the main city newspaper building.

Thies laughed. " 'I wonder who would . . . do something like that, right under Gestapo's noses?' "

"I thought, perhaps for the hundredth time, that the reason we worked so well together was that we thought along similar lines and always recognized a good scheme," Niels recalled. "Finishing our beer, we worked out the details of the plan."

It was daring and unexpected. It just might work.

■ ■ ■

Niels and Thies had contacts with skippers, boat owners, and other resistance workers. Spreading the word, they recruited a retired harbor pilot, a perfect skipper for the secret operation. Then they found a boat that looked enough like the regular canal boats to use. Not wanting to push their luck, they decided to make a quick strike: Their rescue operation would run for two days only.

And that's what they did, ferrying groups of a dozen or fewer throughout each day. Niels recalled the tension building as the very last group was about to board a canal boat to take them to a fishing boat waiting in the harbor.

"I stood at the iron railing bordering the canal and watched a family of four arrive and apprehensively sit down some fifty feet away on the bench for waiting passengers. The man was clutching a pair of gloves in his left hand, our recognition sign," Niels wrote later. "The woman was talking to their two children, barely of school age, who each carried a school bag. Clever, I thought, for we had given strict instructions not to carry suitcases, a sure giveaway to a German observer. The school bags were natural, however, and probably held a few necessities.

"The family looked for all the world to be ordinary citizens, which indeed they were, waiting for a canal boat as part of the normal daily street scene."

In the distance, Niels spotted Thies approaching with three more people. A minute later all waited uneasily on the bench. Then "their" canal boat approached around the bend.

"Thies came over to me and lit a cigarette. 'Last batch,' he mumbled.

"I nodded. As the boat put in to the landing below us, I looked at the people on the bench, then turned and spat in the water. That was our stipulated signal to indicate that this was the boat they should take. They all got up, trooped down the stone steps to the landing and aboard, the children chattering excitedly about the harbor tour they had been told they were taking. A moment later, they were all gone."

■ ■ ■

While Niels was aware that other people were also involved in rescuing the Jews, it wasn't until after the war that he understood the full scope of the extraordinary effort.

Niels reflected on those tense October weeks. As soon as whispers about the roundup of the Jews spread, "a loose network came into being almost overnight to hide the Jews. The rescue effort involved many small resistance groups but was implemented on a large scale by ordinary citizens, people who would never have thought of undertaking sabotage but who rallied to this humanitarian cause without hesitation."

THE RESCUE

Like her brother Jørgen, Elsebet Kieler felt compelled to protest the occupation of her country. Elsebet had strong pacifist ideals and didn't believe in violence. Although the apartment she shared with her brothers and sister had come to be, as she called it, a "general headquarters" for the resistance, her conscience wouldn't allow her to take part in sabotage actions.

But Elsebet *could* help Jewish families get out of harm's way.

Jewish families would need to rely on fishermen and boat owners for transportation. They would also need money. "The costs involved not only the payments to the fishermen, who needed, among other things, a certain guarantee sum for their boats, which could get confiscated, but there were also bribes for the German guard posts and the Danish coastguard," Jørgen explained.

That's where Elsebet started her efforts. Elsebet and Klaus Rønholt, a friend from home and fellow member of their *Frit Danmark* student group, decided to raise money to help finance the rescue operation and pay fishermen.

In their hometown of Horsens, Elsebet and Klaus went from farm to farm collecting donations from prominent landowners. At first the two were met with confusion when they appeared on the doorstep. "'Our various hosts . . . thought we were doing the rounds on account of being engaged, until they were informed otherwise,'" recalled Elsebet. At one house they suddenly found themselves the center of attention at a dinner party.

" 'You handle the ladies,' said Klaus, upon which he strode toward the lounge where the gentlemen were gathered. So there I stood in my sensible clothing, surrounded by elegant ladies—and of course became, as did Klaus, the sensation of the evening.

" 'It was somewhat naïve of us to ride round like we did, entrusting our little secret to all those we met; but on that occasion, our naïveté happened to prove our strength. It disarmed people's resistance,' " said Elsebet.

While Elsebet and Klaus gathered donations, another friend, Ebba Lund, took on the task of finding fishermen willing to use their boats to transport refugees. "Ebba was good at convincing people and another thing that did not do any harm was that she could promise payments in cash—half before sailing, half after receiving a report that the Jews had arrived safely," said Jørgen. "Over the period of a few days, we managed to assemble a flotilla of seven to ten fishing cutters that were ready to sail."

The next step was to get the word out to the Jewish community. Jørgen and Elsebet's parents sent them the first Jewish couple. Ebba's parents got involved too. They hid thirty refugees in their home, and then Ebba helped the families get safely across to Sweden. Ebba became so well known for her efforts that she earned the nickname Girl with the Red Cap, or sometimes simply Red Hat.

The first successful crossing the group organized took place in early October 1943. As the weeks went by and more

The Danish people turn over a German prisoner van and release their fellow citizens.

families left, Jørgen and his friends scoured the city to ensure that every Jewish family needing to escape had a chance to do so. They passed the word among friends and even looked in backyards and alleys in case someone might still be hiding out. People came to them too.

"Once we had become established our reputation followed our success, and a number of people actively sought us and 'our' fishermen out while others were redirected to us by larger organizations that did not have enough boats," said Jørgen. No one was refused who did not have money: The contributions Elsebet and Klaus collected ensured that.

"If there were no complications, the trip would take some two hours," Jørgen said. "If German patrol boats turned up, the vessels had to do some fishing to avoid arousing suspicion, and this could make the journey much longer. The passengers had to keep out of sight until the boat was in Swedish waters." Jørgen estimated that he and his friends helped between five hundred and a thousand people escape successfully.

Mostly it went smoothly, though Ebba recalled one tense encounter. "'One day, I remember it was afternoon and shadows were growing longer, we had gotten some passengers into some of the boats, and they were under deck, and the engine was running, when a German patrol . . . came along the path.'"

Ebba was the only woman among two dozen or so fishermen. She knew the situation looked suspicious. Thinking quickly, she pretended one of the men was her boyfriend. "'I moved close to a young burly fisherman and looked as romantic as I could—given the circumstances. The Germans—some five in all—did not say anything, but stopped and looked on. . . . They also looked at me.

" 'Then they turned and went. I'm absolutely convinced that they knew what was going on, but understood that they would pay dearly, were they to start interfering. It was the eye contact that did it; I will never forget it. Anyway, the boats sailed off and everything went well.' "

■ ■ ■

Rescuers came from all walks of life—even the police. Knud Dyby was a young police officer who tried to use his position to support the resistance. During the occupation he recruited people to distribute illegal newspapers, helped to find volunteers willing to hide freedom fighters in their apartments, distracted German guards during sabotage attacks, and sometimes procured guns or hand grenades.

Said Knud: " 'We did as much as we could to make life miserable for the Germans.' "

When a colleague asked Knud for assistance in getting a Jewish neighbor to safety, he was ready to help. Luckily his boss, aware of the rescue efforts under way, was sympathetic when Knud asked for time off because his grandmother had died—*again*! His boss responded, " 'Don't you think your grandmother would appreciate it if you used a police car?' "

Knud did not use the police car but did meet his friend that evening at a local chocolate shop. The man had brought not just one neighbor but several families and children, all dressed in warm layers. They had boxes and suitcases with them. Right away, Knud realized they'd have to split up. "'I knew the Gestapo would easily spot them and figure out that they were trying to escape.'"

Knud arranged for the group to separate and be escorted by other resistance volunteers to a secret location, where taxi drivers took them to the harbor. Knud knew a helpful fisherman and arranged passage for everyone.

That was the beginning. In an age before cell phones, Knud worked stealthily in the coming weeks. Through word of mouth he connected refugees and fishermen willing to help. Sometimes messages were even left with friendly coworkers at the police station where he worked. "'Somebody always seemed to know somebody in the chain of helpers.'"

The fishermen did charge for their services, though Knud negotiated to keep costs low and cover fuel. His main contact, a good-humored man named Bernhard Ingemann-Andersen, who went by Aage, "'was a poor fisherman with a small half-open boat, always helpful and daring and sometimes he would even borrow bigger boats when he worked for us,'" Knud recalled. "'I would make contact with him by phone, in guarded terms, of course, and then we'd meet at some inn where we could get a schnapps . . . to back up our courage.'"

Once, Knud was asked to help a young officer in the Danish army, who was half Jewish. Aage agreed to take the passenger as a free guest but asked Knud to come along since his usual helper was sick.

"'Then I realized I had a little problem. All the fishing skippers I knew were fairly short of stature, rugged in appearance, with wind-cracked skin darkened by the outdoors and faces always in need of a shave,'" said Knud. Also, most had "'worn-down fingernails on big red hands. I on the other hand was tall, blond, blue-eyed, clean-shaven and pink-faced, with well manicured hands.'"

The answer was obvious: Knud would transform himself into a fisherman. "'I didn't shave for 24 hours, then donned heavy black pants, a turtle-neck sweater, skipper hat and rubber boots.'"

They smuggled the young officer onto the boat "'in the darkness of a typical miserable cold Danish night. Along with his little package of personal belongings, he was squeezed into the fishing boat's small cabin, already filled with nets, fishing tackle, tools, dried-out seaweed, worms and dead fish.

"'In the night, with no running lights and hardly any harbor marking lights, we headed out. I stood next to Aage in his half-open cockpit, on a couple of rough boards almost on top of the diesel motor. Everything was in poor condition, including the motor and the quality of the fuel, but Aage had a fantastic sense of humor, he was adventuresome and daring and his enthusiasm seemed to override the faulty equipment and the old boat. . . . The waves were on the rough side and I was drenched in the old and worn oil-skin coat, which might have fit Aage's helper, but definitely not me. I had the wheel while Aage was busy with some rope and fish hooks. We set the course on an old, cheap compass. . . .

"'In the gray morning light we knew we were in Swedish territory and our passenger could feel free and safe. I do not think he had the feeling of any great freedom—he was dirty, wet, cold. . . . We convinced him to drink some terrible coffee from a thermos.' "

Leaving their passenger with Swedish customs, Aage and Knud headed back. Aage stopped to fish in case their boat was searched. Knud was unable to shake his sense of unease.

" 'Although I was dressed as a fisherman, and miserably wet, unshaven and uncombed, I was more nervous than I had ever been. I felt absolutely stupid and I was sure that if we were boarded the Germans would laugh themselves silly with me claiming to be a fisherman. I knew I would end up with the Gestapo who would interrogate me and in time find that I was a police officer and involved in some resistance activities.' "

Knud determined to leave the ferrying to the skippers after that. Another rule was to avoid learning the names of those he helped. " 'I purposely did not write down any names. I tried not to remember any names if I heard them. It was a risk to know something, and I did not want to know anything more than I had to know, in case I was caught by the Gestapo and they questioned me.' "

In reflecting on his rescue work, Knud later said, " 'Surely, you felt as uneasy and apprehensive as the refugees, but then you felt the compassion and strength, and you knew that they were the ones who had to flee from their previous comfortable existence, their homes and business, to go to a completely unknown future.' "

Knud believed only one thing mattered: to guide as many people as he could " 'away from the Nazi madmen, away from arrest and away from Germany's deadly concentration camps.'"

...

As for young Herbert Pundik, who'd received the warning while at school, he and his family had fled their apartment that night, leaving behind almost everything they owned. After spending one night with friends, they managed to get a taxi to the coastal village of Sletten. There they hid in the home of a fisherman.

"We were sitting in our hiding place with the fisherman in Sletten, cut off from the rest of the world. The fisherman had gone down to the harbor to find out whether anyone wanted to sail across The Sound. He returned without having accomplished his objective. . . . We thought we were all alone in the world."

But they were not forgotten. A friend of Herbert's father, whom he knew as Mr. P. Nicolaisen, had been desperately searching for them. Nicolaisen had tracked them as far as the coast. He was an elderly man who used a cane, yet he walked for miles, house to house, looking for his friend.

Herbert said, "The odds were poor, but he would never have found peace if he had not done his best to save us from the Germans. In the late afternoon there was a knock on our door. We rushed into our hiding places: under the beds, in a closet, behind a door.

"'My name is Nicolaisen,' a voice said. 'I am looking for the Pundik family. Have you seen them at all?'"

CHAPTER TWENTY

At first the fisherman said no, fearing that the stranger was an informer. Luckily Herbert's father recognized his friend's voice and came forward. Later that night, the family was driven along back roads to Mr. Nicolaisen's house, also on the coast.

Herbert recalled what happened next. "Nicolaisen found a fisherman who was willing to sail us across, and the following night we crept across the Strand Road and down to the beach where the fisherman was waiting with a dinghy. His boat was 100 meters further out.

"I remember the last glimpse I caught of the coast before being ordered below. On the beach Nicolaisen and his wife and the fisherman's wife were kneeling in the morning twilight. Their folded hands were lifted toward the sky."

Herbert looked at his watch as they set off. Just thirty-seven minutes later they had passed into Swedish territorial waters. "A Swedish patrol boat hailed us, and we were allowed to come up on deck.

" 'Welcome,' the Swedish sailors called out."

Herbert's escape had taken four days. The Pundik family went to Malmo, Sweden, where Herbert's parents rented an apartment and his father began looking for a job. A week after his headmaster had appeared in the door of his class, Herbert found himself back in school again. Herbert and his family remained in Sweden for nineteen months before returning home.

■ ■ ■

In all, 7,220 Danish Jews escaped to Sweden, along with 686 of their non-Jewish friends or family members. Most traveled in small groups by boat across the Øresund Sound, aided by friends, acquaintances, and, often, total strangers. The effort also succeeded thanks to the cooperation of Sweden and its people.

But most of all it happened because, spontaneously, individuals took action, coming up with creative ways to raise money, find boats, look out for friends, hide neighbors and acquaintances, and help people reach safety. Denmark was, wrote one historian, "a tiny nation in the grip of an omnipotent conqueror; yet in the very hour when it became stripped of its arms and its democratic rule was violently suspended, it suddenly rose and snatched a handful of Jews out of the very hands of their oppressors and spirited them away to safety in Sweden."

Equality was an important value to the Danes. The Danish Freedom Council called on all citizens to get involved, publishing a proclamation that read in part: " 'Among the Danish people the Jews do not constitute a special class but are citizens to exactly the same degree as all other Danes. . . . We Danes know that the whole population stands behind resistance to the German oppressors. The Council calls on the Danish population to help in every way possible those Jewish fellow citizens who have not yet succeeded in escaping abroad.' "

Neighbors not only helped to hide people and arrange transportation but also ensured that the property families had to leave behind would be protected. One man recounted, " 'Before I left Copenhagen on the 11th of October, 1943, I gave a power of attorney to a neighbor . . . authorizing him to take any steps he thought necessary with regard to all property owned by my wife and myself. Our house was immediately cleared of all furniture and was let to a Danish family. All the furniture was stored at another neighbor's house. . . . These friends likewise took it upon themselves to insure [*sic*] that the house was once more furnished and ready to receive us, upon our happy return home on July 15, 1945.' "

∎ ∎ ∎

David Sompolinsky, whose family had been warned by his classmate Robert Pedersen, did not leave Denmark right away. Instead, he stayed behind helping fellow Jews escape, until he himself was forced to flee to avoid being captured.

David recalled the reaction of his fellow citizens during those tense days. " 'In train, tram or simply in the streets, unknown Danes turned to us and offered their help or gave us money. Once someone gave me a gold ring and once in the train a man took off his coat and asked if I'd take it. . . . I could not refuse. Many Danes who were not active in the rescue operation felt obliged to do something or other. I remember one day that the tram conductor refused to accept my fare. I threw the money into his bag. When I got off he said to me in all sincerity, "I am ashamed." ' "

On April 9, 1940, the Danish people had been plunged into despair by the sudden occupation of their nation. Now, three and a half years later, they had the courage to defy the

Nazis and stand up for values that Denmark held dear: free-dom, tolerance, and justice.

Herbert Pundik put it this way: "The thousands and thousands who helped us reach safety behaved in a way that is hard to define in words. . . . The rescue operation was anonymous; it went on quietly and unspectacularly. There were no generals or privates. People did what was needed.

"As Duckwitz wrote in his diary, 'I know what I must do.'"

CHAPTER TWENTY-ONE
NOT EVERYONE ESCAPED

The rescue of the Danish Jews was a spontaneous, grassroots effort that saved the lives of more than 7,200 men, women, and children. But not everyone escaped.

Although records are incomplete, about twenty people drowned while attempting to cross to Sweden. One rowboat capsized, killing eight people. In another tragic accident, a small boat was rammed by a larger one in dark waters, killing several children.

The roundup of Jewish families, which began on October 1, continued through November. By then a total of 474 people had been captured and deported. (Sources disagree on the exact numbers.) Some people were arrested at home, while others were seized as they tried to make their way to boats, or were turned in by informers while hiding out.

Ten people arrested initially were released right away; about 464 Danes were taken to Theresienstadt concentration camp, in the town of Terezín, located in what is now the Czech Republic, where they would spend the next nineteen months. The camp, opened in 1940, was established in what had been a small fortress to protect the town.

Metha and Hirsch Simson and their two children were among those Danes captured. Describing her arrival at Theresienstadt, Metha wrote, "'We were shown into some rooms, or rather an attic, where there were some wooden bunks without bedclothes. The men were by themselves, and the women and children together. We put the children on the bunks and covered them with our coats. The children said they couldn't sleep because it itched, and when I looked I discovered bedbugs and fleas crawling all over them.

"'Not only was there no wood stove, but some of the roof tiles were missing, so there was a nasty cold draft everywhere. The next day Rita complained that she had a sore throat, and Benny cried due to earache. I myself had frightful pains in my stomach.'"

Metha landed in the camp hospital with an ulcer, but the conditions were no better there. "'One night, when I had to go into the hall of the hospital, I met a frightful sight. All those who had died during the night had been thrown out there. There were many. I couldn't stand it any longer, and I applied to return 'home' to the attic. After a three month stay in the hospital, I was allowed to leave.'"

■ ■ ■

Leo Gurewitch had somehow become separated from his family during their escape attempt from Denmark. His wife was able to get away, while his one-year-old daughter was hidden with a foster family in a village. He had been caught while hiding in a church loft.

Leo managed to hold on to a small pocket calendar he used as a diary, hoping that if he didn't survive, his wife might someday read his words. He wrote often of how much he missed them: "'Tonight it is lovely spring weather, and I long

The gate to the Theresienstadt concentration camp in what is now the Czech Republic. Jews from all over Europe, including Denmark, were imprisoned in Theresienstadt, and many thousands were sent on from there to other concentration camps and killing sites.

terribly for you. . . . At night I wake at three or four o'clock and I think about you and our child. Rosa, if you had any idea how I suffer.'"

■ ■ ■

Mélanie Oppenhejm; her husband, Morits; and two of her children, seventeen-year-old Ellen and eighteen-year-old Ralph, were also captured on October 1. Beginning in the 1930s, as the persecution of Jews intensified in Germany, Mélanie had been active in efforts to bring Jewish children to safety in Denmark and other countries. Now she and her family were facing the same fate from which she'd worked so hard to save others.

Packed into cattle trucks on the way to the camp, Mélanie and her family could barely grasp what was happening to them. They had gone from normal lives and comfortable homes to experiencing a horrific nightmare. "The floorboards were strewn with muck. We could neither sit nor lie down. Some people fainted, others were in a state of shock. They could not comprehend what had befallen them; it was all so grotesquely unreal—to be simply carted away like a sack of potatoes."

Mélanie was appalled at what she saw when they arrived. "Forty thousand people were, unbelievably, crammed into that camp. . . . We saw nothing but emaciated faces; we heard nothing but noise. . . . And now we encountered people who appeared to be moving at an unimaginably slow pace, as if in slow motion. We were at a loss to understand: why did all those thousands of people walk in such a peculiar way?

What was the matter with them? Well, they were hungry. They just could not walk any faster."

It wasn't long before Mélanie herself was suffering from the effects of the thin, revolting soup that she and the other prisoners were given. "I well remember, about two weeks later, standing at the top of some stairs and looking down. I thought: how do I get down there? Of course, I did get down. I had to, because we were forced to go to work. But we had become so enfeebled."

• • •

Incredibly Leo Gurewitch, the Simson family, and the Oppenhejms all survived, in part because the Danish people did not forget their fellow citizens who'd been taken away. The effort to intercede on behalf of Danish prisoners involved the Danish Red Cross, officials in Danish government departments such as social welfare, an aid committee based in Stockholm, Sweden, and many individuals. Werner Best, probably for his own political reasons, received assurances from Germany that the Danish prisoners would stay in Theresienstadt and not be sent to more notorious death camps. (Scholars continue to debate Best's motivation and the rather complicated role he played.)

Efforts to help those who had been deported included arranging for the shipping of clothing parcels, which began in December 1943, as well as pressuring the Germans to allow for the delivery of food parcels, something which went against official policy. Dr. Richard Ege, a specialist in nutrition, worked with Danish drug companies to produce special multivitamins to be sent to the prisoners, although Mélanie Oppenhejm remembered that vitamin pills had to be handed over. "They would be sent back to Denmark as evidence that we had no need of such things."

The first food parcels were shipped in February 1944. Since many people of Jewish descent had no relatives left at home in Denmark, others stepped in to organize the parcels and compile a list of names so that no one would be forgotten.

The prisoners' correspondence was censored; Mélanie remembered not being allowed to write more than twenty-five words every month. She described making hidden appeals for food. For instance, a postcard might say, "'Greetings to Mathilde Christensen!'" or "'All the best to Rubow!'" Christensen's was a delicatessen and Rubow a bakery in Copenhagen. The postcards contained a hidden meaning: We are hungry; please help.

The food parcels that reached the prisoners had often been opened and pilfered. Sometimes they contained bugs. Even so, they had an impact. Wrote Mélanie, "Life for us was totally transformed. . . . There was a rule which prevented us from receiving more than one parcel per month, and frequently it would be only half a parcel. Even the fat in a sausage could be of immeasurable value, if one cherished any hopes of survival."

The Danes continued to put pressure on Germany to ensure better conditions for Danish citizens, pressing for the right to visit the camp. Germany, which still depended on some shipments from Denmark, was more likely to negotiate

Prisoners in the Theresienstadt concentration camp after its liberation in 1945.

with Danish demands with regard to prisoners than any from other countries.

On July 23, 1944, Danish officials and representatives of the International Red Cross visited. Tragically it appears that in order to show off Theresienstadt, which was supposedly "a model camp," the Nazis sent more than 7,500 non-Danish prisoners to other, even more heinous concentration camps.

The visit was a heartbreaking experience for the Danish prisoners in other ways too. Mélanie recalled that the camp was "embellished" with fresh paint and the addition of little shops displaying meat and vegetables. It was, of course, all a lie. During the visit, the Danes were ordered to give no hint of the true conditions. The visitors, recalled Mélanie, had "no means of penetrating the web of intrigue and make-believe."

CHAPTER TWENTY-ONE

The horrific truth was hidden. Still, there can be no doubt that the pressure from Denmark made some difference in the lives of the Danish Jews in Theresienstadt. Danish prisoners were allowed to live together as families, to receive food packages that helped with the effects of starvation, and to hold out hope they had not been forgotten.

Survivor Rabbi Max Friediger, the chief rabbi of the Jewish community in Denmark, had been arrested and imprisoned in August and then sent to Theresienstadt. Writing about the impact of food parcels, he said, "'The mind was fortified by the wonderful realization that at home they were thinking of us and working for us.

"'For—so we thought—when those at home take care that we shall not starve to death, then they will also find ways and means of delivering us from this hell.'"

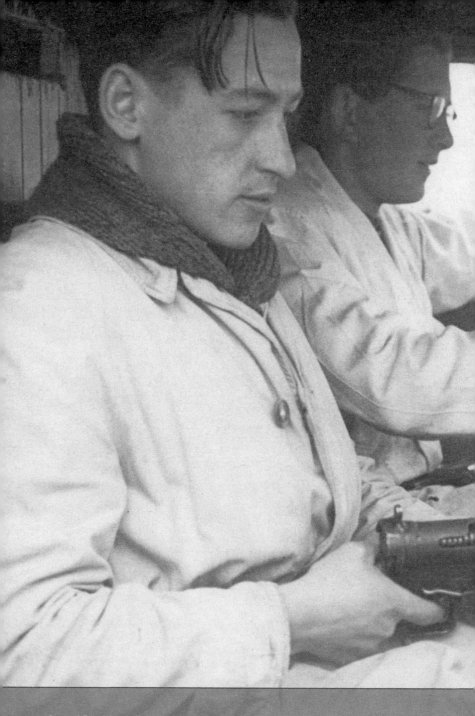
Armed Danish civilians struggle against the occupying forces during World War II.

PART THREE

ACTION & ARREST
FALL 1943–SUMMER 1944

Many times during the past two days I've thought of how wonderful it was to live at home with you and enjoy all the things that home has to give. . . . There are so many things which you can see and understand only after being separated from others. I share this cell with five other fellows, and we have lively discussions about everything under the sun.

—Kim Malthe-Bruun, December 21, 1944
(arrested December 19, 1944)

arrest (v): to catch, capture, seize, lay hold upon.

CHAPTER TWENTY-TWO

HD2 IN ACTION

By the fall of 1943, Jørgen Kieler was leading a double life. Along with his siblings, he continued to attend lectures, keeping up with his medical studies as best he could. The Kielers still lived in their same apartment and went openly about their everyday activities. Yet they all spent more and more time on secret resistance work—printing underground newspapers, smuggling Jewish families out of the country, and conducting sabotage operations.

Jørgen's resolve to defy the Germans was heightened after the crackdown on Jews in October 1943. He made contact with other resistance leaders, including a man named Jens Lillelund, code name Finn, a member of the sabotage group Holger Danske. Named after a folktale hero, Holger Danske (Ogier the Dane in English) included legendary saboteurs such as Flammen (the Flame) and Citronen (the Lemon).

Several active members of Holger Danske had recently been forced to flee to Sweden. Finn approached Jørgen to see if the young student and his friends would be willing to help continue the effort by forming a sabotage group to be called Holger Danske 2, or HD2.

Jørgen jumped at the chance to keep the spirit of the folk hero alive, especially since, according to legend, Holger Danske "would come to Denmark in her hour of need." Now was the time for Holger Danske to return.

HD2 became a loosely knit group of naval cadets and

students. Four women took part, including Nan Møller, Jørgen's childhood friend from their hometown of Horsens. His sisters, Bente and Elsebet, helped behind the scenes. While at the time, as Jørgen reflected later, sabotage itself "was considered a man's job," these young women also put themselves on the line. A courting couple might be less noticeable during surveillance of a possible sabotage site. The group all met together, often in the Kielers' apartment, to make plans and discuss strategies. If arrested, gender wouldn't matter. The women, Jørgen noted, "were fully aware of the fact that the death penalty awaited anyone who accommodated or otherwise helped the saboteurs."

"'Our friends marveled at the fact that we did not go underground,'" Elsebet wrote, "'but we needed somewhere to meet, a home where we could live a normal mental life, because the work itself embraced values that could almost knock us off our feet, and which we all felt represented a concrete power within us.'"

The shadow of possible capture always hung over them. "We considered this life 'above ground' as good camouflage, something which would fool the enemy," said Jørgen. "It was nevertheless evident that this sham could only be maintained so long as none of us got arrested. Code names and forged documents obviously became part and parcel of our everyday lives."

An SOE agent named Erik Jens Peter Petersen, who went by Jens Peter, provided some training to the group. He'd been dropped in by parachute on July 25, 1943, by the SOE to be a sabotage instructor to support the growing number of resistance groups. He managed to remain active without being captured through the end of the war.

Jørgen found his first training session with the experienced saboteur a little frightening. "Jens Peter did not beat about the bush," Jørgen said. "Out of his bag he pulled detonators, fuses, ignition equipment . . . plus various types of bombs and explosives. This was spread out on the table and so the lesson began. I felt that it was something of a miracle that we did not all get blown up on the spot."

Jørgen also made contact with another experienced freedom fighter named Svend Otto Nielsen, who went by the nickname John. HD2 kept in touch with John and the SOE through a bookshop in the center of the city. While HD2 didn't have to take specific orders from the British, the SOE was now playing a stronger role in coordinating sabotage actions and selecting targets, just as Ralph Hollingworth had always envisioned. John was active in HD2 operations and served as the group's liaison with the SOE. He became a close friend, inspiration, and mentor to Jørgen.

After three practice attempts, members of HD2 were ready for their first operation on Sunday, November 7, 1943. The afternoon before, Jørgen and John had traveled to do reconnaissance at the target the SOE had selected for sabotage: a radio factory producing equipment for the Germans.

The plan seemed straightforward enough. Wearing a Danish police uniform, Jørgen would ring the bell at the gate and ask to inspect the factory's blackout plans. John would follow him inside, distract the guards, and someone else would place explosives.

CHAPTER TWENTY-TWO

Nothing went right. Instead of opening the gate, the guard shone a flashlight down on Jørgen's head from a second-floor window, demanding that he identify himself. Jørgen tried to bluff his way out of the situation. Suspicious, the guard ordered him to stay where he was or be shot. Suddenly Jørgen heard a faint whistle from the street. Seeing that he was in trouble, John ran up and shot out a spotlight so Jørgen could make his escape.

The attempt was a failure. To make matters worse, they'd run off leaving the explosives behind, which were hidden in a backpack under a hedge. Luckily they were able to retrieve it the next day without being noticed.

Two nights later, HD2 tried again. This time, instead of attempting to gain access to sabotage the actual machinery, the saboteurs decided to attack from the outside, with the goal of destroying the entire factory. Four group members acted as guards, while others—the bomb unit—ran up to the windows and smashed them, shouting a warning to anyone still inside. A small explosive was thrown first, to be sure any guards or workers took the warning seriously. Once the building was empty, the larger bomb was detonated, setting off a fiery blaze. No one was hurt, and the factory was consumed by fire.

A few weeks later, Jørgen had another close call. Following a failed sabotage attempt, the group split up after being fired on by German soldiers. Running alone, Jørgen was stopped by a Danish policeman who took his pistol but seemed uncomfortable, unsure of what to do with his prisoner.

"I informed him that he had the choice of letting me escape or taking me to the police station, which would mean

A store in Copenhagen is set on fire by demonstrators in an act of sabotage in 1944.

I would be handed over to the Germans and executed," said Jørgen.

John arrived in time to help, though it seemed the policeman intended to let Jørgen go. (The police officer kept the pistol and, years after the war, tracked Jørgen down to return it.)

Several close calls like these led to a sleepless night of soul-searching for the young activist. Yes, he was afraid. There was the fear of arrest and torture, of hurting innocent people, of not being able to handle the unexpected. There was also, of course, the fear of dying.

"I had gone into the struggle with my eyes open, knowing full well that it could cost me my life, and I was prepared, in principle, to pay the price." What Jørgen feared most, he realized, was losing "all sense of proportion," losing his sense of the value of a human life.

After staying awake all night, Jørgen decided it was time to put his doubts aside. "Otherwise I would never be able to do an effective job."

Their mission was just. Despite the danger, he would keep on.

■ ■ ■

For a while, things went smoothly and HD2 had a string of successes. One priority was to target factories; any disruption to the German war machine could save lives elsewhere. The group set fire to a factory making German uniforms, and to another that produced sound locators used for pinpointing British aircraft.

Informers were a constant threat. In early December, two agents who were helpful to HD2 found themselves in grave danger. Jens Lillelund, code name Finn, who'd originally contacted Jørgen about forming the group, and Jørgen's friend John (Svend Otto Nielsen) were given a supposedly safe place to stay for the night by a new contact. The woman betrayed them.

Later, Jørgen was able to piece together what happened. As the two resistance activists set off on their bicycles the next morning, Germans began shooting at them. Finn managed to escape, but John was seriously wounded and taken away. Jørgen and the others heard about the incident but for months would not learn if John was dead or alive.

"John's arrest obviously made a deep impression on us. We thought he was dead but had no accurate information about what had happened to him," said Jørgen.

Despite this frightening setback, no one in HD2 was ready to give up. HD2 was able to make contact with another agent at the SOE to help identify targets and get access to sabotage materials. As a result of the heightened danger and difficulty of getting explosives in the city, the group began to take on more assignments outside Copenhagen. As HD2's reputation for successful actions became known, the group became "a flying squad," traveling to other areas to conduct sabotage.

One prime target was the Varde Steelworks on the peninsula of Jutland. Danish resistance fighters had learned that the British were interested in having the factory destroyed. If it couldn't be done from the ground, planes might be sent in. But an air attack carried other risks. Since the factory was located in the middle of town, "an aerial bombardment would have cost the lives of hundreds of local residents," Jørgen recalled. HD2 would make the attempt.

The action was set for December 12, 1943. Ten HD2 members traveled by train and taxi to Varde, where they met a steelworker and resistance activist named Viggo Hansen. Hansen had made detailed drawings of the factory. After they reviewed the details of the operation, the members set out.

"'When we had agreed on everything, we went two by two over to the steelworks. . . . We entered the compound by cutting our way through the chain-link fencing. The members of

A train derailed by sabotage in Denmark.

HD2 took the four guards completely by surprise in the guard-room when they kicked open the door,'" recalled Hansen. "'The guards did not have time to raise the alarm. . . . The guards voluntarily handed over the keys to the works, after which we locked them in the air raid shelter. . . . The operation was a great success. . . . Production at the steelworks was effectively stopped for some six months.'"

The incident received international coverage. *The New York Times* on December 12, 1943, reported that forty to fifty Danish patriots had overpowered guards to blow up the plant making German arms. "But in reality there were ten," Jørgen said.

The success at the steelworks established HD2 as a leading sabotage squad. The group continued to operate through the end of the year and into the early winter months of 1944. In mid-January, Jørgen and his group sabotaged a large drilling machine in the B&W Engineering Plant, which was doing work for the German army.

Afterward, Jørgen felt sure their efforts were having an impact. "One of the engineers supervising the repair work had told workers to slow down. He commented that as a number of young people had risked their lives to help B&W to avoid having to collaborate with the Germans, there seemed to be no point in hindering this worthy aim by speeding up repair work."

Comments like this encouraged the young saboteurs. It seemed that the resistance was gaining more support from the Danish people every day. The strike and uprising in August, the efforts to help Jewish families escape in October, the continued growth of the underground press, and increased cooperation and organization among resistance groups were all fostering a sense of national unity and purpose. The goal: to overthrow the Germans and disrupt the German war machine as much as possible.

"The B&W operation had been a huge success," Jørgen reflected, "and we had been very lucky."

That luck was about to run out.

OPERATION TWENTY-SIX

By early 1944, Jørgen Kieler and his HD2 group had carried out nearly two dozen sabotage acts. Their twenty-sixth operation was planned for February 6, 1944, at two factories in Aabenraa, a small harbor village in southern Denmark. Run by Danes who were collaborating with the Germans, the Hamag and Callesen factories made parts for U-boats and airplanes. The SOE had selected the target; HD2 was asked to help, since the local resistance group was too small to handle the operation alone.

From the beginning, Jørgen had his doubts. Aabenraa wasn't a big place. A dozen or so newcomers suddenly arriving with large, heavy suitcases were bound to be noticed. And if their luggage was searched, the explosives would, of course, be found. The town's location so close to the German border meant there might be more pro-German informants than usual. With this in mind, Jørgen decided to schedule a visit to the local hospital when he arrived, to inquire about a future job as a doctor. That would at least give him a cover story if anyone asked why he'd come to town.

There were other logistical challenges. The sabotage would take place in the middle of the night, so the resistance fighters would need a safe place to hide out the next day. They anticipated the roads would be watched and the train station would be crawling with Germans.

A fire caused by an act of sabotage rages in a radio factory in Copenhagen in 1944.

CHAPTER TWENTY-THREE

All these factors spelled a dangerous undertaking. "But the operation had been approved by the SOE, so we regarded this as a sign that Britain wanted us to do it and we agreed to cooperate," Jørgen said.

Headquarters would be the home of a local car mechanic, Peter Koch, whose landlady, Laura Lund, was also sympathetic to the cause. On Saturday afternoon, February 6, more than a dozen members of the group rendezvoused there to review plans and the sketches of the factories.

There would be two nearly simultaneous actions. Three HD2 members and three local men were assigned to the Hamag factory, which had no anti-sabotage guards. The goal was to damage lathes, machines used for shaping wood or metal, to make the factory useless.

The rest of the men would be deployed to the Callesen factory. Since it was surrounded by a barricaded gate with two guards, several saboteurs would enter the factory compound from the property next door by climbing over a wall with barbed wire on top. They would then make their way to the building where the guards were located, surprise them, and open the gate for everyone else.

They set out. But when Jørgen and the others arrived at the chosen spot, they found a heap of scrap metal there. It would be almost impossible to climb without making noise. To make matters worse, their local guide got cold feet and disappeared, leaving Jørgen and the others on their own to try to locate the guards.

"We in our group were very familiar with the problem of

fear, and no one would hold it against anyone who dropped out during the planning stage. But once you had committed yourself, then your colleagues' lives were in your hands. And this man had let us down," said Jørgen.

Without the guide, it was hard to know exactly where to go. Jørgen finally found what he thought was the right building. He spied a chink of light shining in the dark. Then the trouble began. "I suddenly heard a voice saying, 'Yes, I'm speaking from Callesen's. Persons unknown have entered the compound.' So now we knew where the guards were, but also that the police had been notified."

The crucial element of surprise was gone. Time was running short. Jørgen faced a choice: Pull out or move ahead. In a few seconds, Jørgen made his decision. He shot off the lock on the door and kicked it open. The guards, unharmed, were lying on the floor. They had only a minute or two before the police arrived. Opening the gate, the group let in the others, who hurried to place explosives around the lathes.

They managed to get the fuses set, light the fuses, and escape. But it didn't work. Danish police and German soldiers arrived in time to prevent the bombs from going off. The operation at the other factory had proceeded flawlessly, but the Callesen attempt had failed. Now all they could do was try to escape. If they'd had several cars, they could have loaded everyone in and sped away. They had no cars.

"We had the choice of wandering around on the roads leading from the village, in order to get to a railway station

CHAPTER TWENTY-THREE

that was not being guarded by the Germans, or hiding somewhere in Aabenraa itself, until the acute danger had passed.
We chose the latter option and therefore beat our retreat and
went to our various lodgings," said Jørgen.

The young men of HD2 were running for their lives.

CHAPTER TWENTY-FOUR

A TRAIL OF BLOOD

In the town of Aabenraa, the Germans were on the lookout for anyone who might have taken part in the sabotage attacks. Jørgen Kieler and other HD2 members were lying low, holed up with various resistance sympathizers. Their best bet was to make their way to railway stations in small groups of two or three, hoping to blend in and not attract notice by local police or German patrols.

Jørgen and five others were staying with Peter Koch, the mechanic, where they'd begun the operation. But rather than leave town, the saboteurs began to discuss other options. HD2 didn't like to fail. Maybe it would be possible to try again.

They decided to risk it. They would let their other friends get safely away first. Then they'd make a second attempt on the Callesen factory. To do this, though, they'd need more explosives.

One member of the group, Jens Jørgensen, volunteered to take the train to a city about fifty miles away to locate more explosives. They set up a coded message system: If he succeeded in finding a contact who could provide sabotage materials, he'd send a telegram to Koch saying "Happy Birthday!" If he couldn't, the telegram would read "Have a nice anniversary."

Jørgensen set off with an empty suitcase. There would be no telegram.

Stopped by the Gestapo at the train station, Jørgensen

was shot in the chest, though he somehow managed to escape into the woods. Miraculously he met three other members of HD2 hiding there, trying to stay out of sight as they waited to board the next train. The four found a taxi to take them away from town. Eventually they all escaped and were able to find a doctor to help Jørgensen.

Jørgen, of course, would not learn all this until much later. While they waited for the telegram, he and four others—Peer Borup, Niels Hjorth, Klaus Rønholt, and Viggo Hansen—went back to a small toolshed behind Koch's house to take stock of their equipment. Suddenly two German cars drove up to the house.

"We knew it must be us they were looking for and loaded our pistols immediately while thinking about what we should do next," Jørgen said.

They had two choices: Stay and shoot, or try to escape through the toolshed window. Then they heard shouts and a gunshot from the main house. Laura Lund was shot as she attempted to distract the Germans from looking in the backyard.

Jørgen made a decision. "We had to get away. Klaus kicked out the window and was badly cut. We clambered out into the garden and ran into the fields around the back of the house. Here I could see Niels and Viggo in front of me and Klaus was a little way behind. I saw a figure disappearing behind a knoll and thought, 'Peer has also managed to escape.' But it was not him."

As they ran across the snow, Klaus shouted, "'Jørgen, look

at my legs!'" He'd been struck by a bullet and cut by window glass.

The four raced for a nearby farmhouse, but the blood staining the white snow was a sure giveaway. Jørgen tried to prop up his friend as they ran. Klaus protested: "'No, Jørgen, I can't manage, everything's going black in front of my eyes. It'd be better if you shot me in the head and got away yourself.'"

Instead, Jørgen scooped him up piggyback-style and stumbled ahead. At the farmhouse, an old woman stared at them and pointed to where four bicycles stood next to a building. They grabbed them, taking turns trying to help Klaus hold on. When they heard a car approach, Jørgen waved the other two on while he bundled Klaus into a ditch to hide. The car passed.

"I still remember it as being a fine winter's day with a severe frost, but no wind," said Jørgen. As he looked at the lovely snow-covered landscape around him, a thought occurred to him about the country he loved: "It was worth fighting for.

"But I had more important things to think about. I set about dressing Klaus's wounds, and ripped my shirt into strips. He had been wounded in both legs. . . . We lay in the ditch for about three quarters of an hour, while Klaus recovered. But we had to move on. It would have been far too easy for them to find us, if we had stayed where we were. As I bandaged Klaus, I discovered that a stray shot had hit me in the fingers. That too was bleeding and all in all, our trail of blood was leading the Germans right to us."

CHAPTER TWENTY-FOUR

Jørgen helped Klaus climb back onto the bike, and they kept on as best they could. From the top of a hill they spotted the railway line in the distance. If they could reach it, they might be able to escape. Spotting another car in the distance, they scrambled back into the ditch to hide.

This time it was too late. The car stopped and voices began shouting at them. They were surrounded by six Germans. Jørgen hid their identity cards under a pile of leaves and stood up, hands in the air.

One of the soldiers asked, "'Where are the other two?'"

They shook their heads, pretending to know nothing. Jørgen spun out a story in German: They'd been attacked by four men who'd been after their identity cards and had shot Klaus in the leg, then proceeded to disappear. The Germans, of course, weren't buying this.

Once again, the soldiers asked about the other two. When Jørgen refused to cooperate, he was struck on the back of the head with a rifle butt. The two prisoners were marched back to the farmhouse, where the bicycles were returned. Then they were loaded onto a truck.

Jørgen recalled, "Klaus lay there shivering. He was in quite a bad way. I took my jacket off to lay over him and then discovered it was full of blood and that there was a hole near the collar. I had been hit by a bullet when I had peered over the edge of the ditch. Now I understood the pains in my back and shoulder, plus the stiffness in my neck."

Jørgen had been shot in the left side of his neck, with the bullet emerging through his right shoulder blade. "It was something of a miracle that my arms and legs had not been paralyzed. But I obviously belong to the type that survives everything. I have had many lives."

Jørgen himself was lucky, yet tragedy had struck. Hjorth and Hansen had managed to escape, first on the borrowed bicycles, then by tramping through fields and back roads until they caught a train home from another town.

Peer Borup had not gotten away. He had been fatally shot in the head by German soldiers while in the toolshed. He was twenty-two years old.

● ● ●

Later that day, after Klaus had been taken to a hospital, Jørgen was surprised to be herded into the back of a German truck with his brother, Flemming, and another HD2 member, Georg Jansen. As it turned out, the two hadn't left town but had instead decided to go see Jørgen and the others earlier that day. On their way, they'd been spotted by an informant and arrested along with Peter Koch, the mechanic who'd been so helpful.

Reunited, the brothers bumped along in the back of the truck, trying desperately to communicate, though they were forbidden by their guards to speak. In the end, all Jørgen could manage was a whisper: " 'Play for time, deny everything as long as possible.' "

Jørgen reflected, "The saboteurs were all prepared for arrest and torture . . . and everybody knew that there is a limit to courage. Therefore, the general instruction was to keep silent for the first twenty-four hours. That would give those who had not yet been arrested a reasonable chance to escape and to continue the fight."

· · ·

On February 10, 1944, HD2 member Peer Borup was buried in Horsens, the Kielers' hometown. Nan Møller, another childhood friend and HD2 activist, wrote about the funeral in her diary: " 'The whole of the town had put the flags out, but the Germans went into the shops and ordered people to take them down again. Everyone wanted to follow him to his grave, but that was prohibited.' "

The Germans continued to search for members of HD2. Both of Jørgen's sisters, Elsebet and Bente, were arrested. In a separate action, his father, Dr. Ernst Kieler, who was involved with the underground press in Horsens, was also taken. Four Kieler siblings—and their father—were now enemy prisoners. The community rallied around the family. Physician friends of his father's in Horsens decided to care for Dr. Kieler's patients while he was in prison and give the money to Jørgen's mother.

Jørgen, his brother, Flemming, and two other HD2 members were transferred to the Vestre Fængsel prison in Copenhagen on February 10, 1944. Eventually both Elsebet and Bente were interned there as well. Their mother brought their youngest sister, Lida, with her to Copenhagen so that she could visit her children in prison and easily send them parcels.

As Jørgen wrote later, "My family and I became very familiar with the Vestre Fængsel prison in Copenhagen."

CHAPTER TWENTY-FIVE
WE FINALLY GOT YOU

Niels Skov had begun doing sabotage as a personal act of defiance, armed with just his homemade screwdriver and a packet of matches. During the past four years, he'd resisted joining a well-formed resistance organization.

There were dangers to a large organization, as Jørgen Kieler and his fellow freedom fighters were finding. The HD2 group included the four Kieler siblings, eleven naval cadets, and seven or eight college friends. While its size gave the group resources to tap when taking on risky sabotage actions, it also increased the risk of more people being discovered and captured if one member of the group was arrested.

Niels preferred to operate with his friend Thies (Carlo Marqvard Thomsen) or within small, independent groups, which he felt would be harder for the Germans to penetrate and destroy. But like Jørgen, Niels had increasingly been drawn more and more into the resistance. He was leading a double life. "My days had turned into a flurry of activity, as I devoted all the time that could be spared from engineering school to various resistance projects. . . . I had also begun to meet requests for instruction sessions for would-be saboteurs."

The appeals for his help "mysteriously seemed to come out of nowhere, always by word of mouth from people with whom I had had some touch, however fleeting." This carried danger, as both Niels and Thies well understood. The more people

CHAPTER TWENTY-FIVE

knew about their resistance activities, the more likely it was they would become known to the Germans or become the target of informers.

Still, he went ahead with the training sessions, which usually involved six people or fewer. Niels never held them in the same place or with the same people. He also began to disguise his name. Except when at home or school, Niels went by Aage Jørgensen. "Jørgensen is a common Danish name, Aage is my middle name. Easy to remember."

One night, Thies and Niels were surprised to find forty-two people at their training session. Niels felt a bit nervous at the large size of the group. Could he be sure there were no informers? At the end, he asked for a three-minute head start so he could leave alone. Picking up his briefcase, he walked to the streetcar.

Luckily he wasn't followed then. But just like HD2, Niels and Thies had run out of luck.

■ ■ ■

Niels had followed his conscience; he was an ordinary citizen who'd begun doing extraordinary things. Despite his successful operations, involvement in the underground press, and bold plan to help with the rescue of Danish Jews, in the end, like so many others, he was an untrained amateur.

In late May 1944, Niels wasn't able to reach Thies by phone. He went by his friend's parents' house. They'd devised a prearranged signal: If a geranium in an old porcelain pot was missing, something was wrong. The plant was not there. Over the next couple of days, Niels learned that several of the resistance fighters he and Thies knew had been arrested. Did that mean that Thies had also been taken?

The latest issue of their underground newssheet, *The Home Front* (*Hjemmefronten*), was in the process of being printed, and Niels wondered what to do next. If he were the only one left in the group, it would be up to him to get it distributed. On May 26, Niels called a friend to arrange transportation for the newssheets after they were printed.

"Then I went to the print shop . . . where I found that the issue was ready. The printer's name was R. Markussen. He was a small, rat-faced man with close-set eyes that seemed to cast dark glances in all directions simultaneously. He told me in a nervous half whisper that Thies had been there four days earlier and had mentioned that some of our group had been caught. The man's behavior should have alerted me, but nervous people were only too common, and as this guy knew of some of the arrests, his fear seemed natural enough."

Niels left. Just as he was stepping off the curb at the intersection, the printer's words began ringing in his mind. Something bothered him. Then it came to him in a flash: "Thies would not have told him about the others being arrested!"

The printer had betrayed them. (Later, Niels was to learn that Thies had been arrested in the print shop itself.) Niels was still crossing the intersection as the pieces of the puzzle began to fall into place.

It was already too late.

When he was halfway across the street, a man stopped in front of him, stuck a pistol in his face, and hissed at him in

CHAPTER TWENTY-FIVE

German to put his hands up. Two other men fell on Niels, twisting his arms together and forcing them into handcuffs.

Beside them a car appeared, its back door open. "I was shoved into it with a man on each side and one on top of me, and we sped off as quickly as traffic allowed. The entire operation took fewer than forty-five seconds, and we were gone before people in the street realized what was happening. I was in the hands of professionals."

The car sped to Dagmarhus, an office building across from city hall that German security police had taken over for their headquarters. This is where the interrogation of Danish prisoners took place.

Niels was brought to an office and shoved into a chair, across from a German officer who lit a cigar. "'Well, Aage Jørgensen, we finally got you.'" The man spoke in German, which another agent translated into Danish.

Niels understood German well enough. But he played along and answered in Danish, "'No, you didn't. . . . My name is Niels Skov, so you have the wrong man.'"

The agent smiled and pointed to a thick file on his desk. "'We will now put your real name on this and get started.'"

As he sat there, Niels realized he'd never thought through exactly what might happen if he did get caught. He and Thies and the other activists he knew had all been gambling. "We were in the truest sense of the word amateur players in a game where our lives were the ante and where the rules heavily favored the house. I saw in a flash that my own attitude had been a mixture of arrogance and naïveté in assuming that my charmed career could go on forever."

Niels couldn't help wondering, "Did they have enough on me to shoot me? That question was soon answered, for as they dug into my file it became readily apparent that they had enough on me to shoot me several times over."

Niels quickly realized that the officers wanted information: "names and details that could lead them toward further arrests. I, on my part, wanted time. After all, every new day held the promise of something—anything—to change the situation. I might escape. Or the war might end. Or Hitler might drop dead."

Suddenly, impatient with his silence, the officer with the cigar walked over and looked down at Niels. Then the man "reached over and slowly stubbed out his cigar on the back of my hand in the soft area between thumb and index finger. The pain was briefly excruciating, surging through my body, and despite my extreme effort to prevent it, tears filled my eyes. There was an ugly black spot on my hand, and I smelled burning flesh, *my* flesh . . . and in a rush my anger far overcame the pain."

The officer said, " 'Maybe now you would like to talk?'

"I waited, pretending not to understand until it was translated, then hissed my reply at the interpreter.

" 'You'd better tell him he'll need lots of cigars.' "

. . .

Later that night, Niels was brought to Vestre Fœngsel, the same prison where Jørgen Kieler was being held. "Two prison guards led me to a small cell, told me to undress and to lie down on a steel cot hinged to the wall, cuffed my hands together and chained them to the cot, and left me with lights on and a guard outside who checked on me randomly and frequently. . . . I closed my eyes and reviewed my situation, and for the first time I did feel really *CAUGHT*. I was absolutely, totally unable to do anything except lie like a lump of meat and wait for somebody else to make the next move."

That first shock of captivity made an indelible impression. "It was a completely new, alien experience to be locked up with my hands chained to a metal cot," Niels reflected years later.

"The coarse blankets were scratchy, the chains were cutting my wrists, and the charred spot on my left hand throbbed in protest against the cigar treatment. I now knew exactly what freedom was: it was what I had just stupidly lost."

IN THE "HOTEL VESTRE": NIELS SKOV

Four years earlier, Jørgen Kieler and Niels Skov had been young idealistic students struggling with how to respond to the enemy in their midst. Their commitment to fighting the Nazis had led them to decisions that had landed them in prison. Along the way, other friends had been arrested or killed. Now they faced the hard realization that they too might die for their beliefs.

They held on to the hope that the Allies would soon defeat Germany. The week after Niels was arrested, on June 6, 1944, D-day took place. The Allied Expeditionary Force landed more than 160,000 troops in Normandy, France. That same day, outside Copenhagen, fifty saboteurs from the BOPA group blew up a major target, the Globus factory, which made airplane rudders for German war planes. This was a significant victory that caused major damage, and the Allies were grateful that the factory had been put out of commission. But although the tide was turning and the Allies were gaining ground every day, that didn't mean the war was over. Prisoners like Niels and Jørgen could still face execution.

Niels found himself confined to a bare cell, where he was given a piece of rye bread and a mug of weak coffee for breakfast. Pulling himself up to the one small window with its two steel bars, he looked out on the empty prison yard. That day, and for days after, Niels was taken to headquarters for interrogation. He divided his brain into two parts: One dealt with his daily routine of eating, sleeping, and interrogation. "The other branch, the important one, devoted full time to planning escape. . . . Always, always and everywhere, the idea of escape dominated my consciousness."

It did not look promising. This was no makeshift temporary holding building; it had been built as a prison before the war. Niels and the other prisoners were surrounded by concrete and steel bars. He was still being taken to the fourth floor of Gestapo headquarters for questioning each day. Each day he found himself wondering whether he could somehow break through a window, jump to the sidewalk, and survive. It didn't seem likely.

The worst part was traveling to and from the interrogation. "In downtown traffic we waited obediently at stop lights where I found myself a tantalizing four feet from carefree people on bicycles: craftsmen, office workers, students, housewives, sun-tanned girls—all of them my countrymen, not one of whom wished me dead."

But not one of them could help.

Niels maintained an unwavering focus on escape. That helped to motivate him to stay in good physical shape despite the poor food and lack of exercise. Although his wrists were chained in his cell, after a little practice he learned how to squeeze out of the chain once the guard left for the night. He did chin-ups on the window ledge and, after two weeks, could do them one-handed.

Soon Niels noticed a slight change in prison routine. The prisoners were now allowed a half hour of exercise each morning. Well, most of them anyway. Niels was forced to sit in his cell as he heard the other cell doors open. One morning, a guard swung his door open too and stood there, checking a list in his hand. While Niels waited for instructions, he watched other prisoners filing past. "Suddenly, there was Thies, in view for less than two seconds only fifteen feet away! He looked at me sideways without changing his facial expression of detached boredom."

The next day, the same thing happened. Though he was not allowed to join the others, Niels's cell door was opened. This time, Thies tossed a tiny ball of paper toward his friend as he walked by. Niels quickly covered it with his foot. Later he was able to read the note that had been scribbled on rough toilet paper:

" 'Well, this . . . guard obviously made a mistake by exposing you to the cruel world thru an open door but hoping he will be as stupid tomorrow I'll send you this and if you have something to write with we'll set up regular mail service on top of the cistern above the toilet in the second stall . . . look there and leave me a note . . . I don't know why they honor you with that chain on your wrists but by all means don't let it go to your head . . .' "

Knowing that Thies was still alive, his sense of humor intact, gave Niels a little hope. The Gestapo informed him interrogations were over. All that remained was for Niels to be sentenced for the accusations against him. These included destruction of German war material, printing and distributing illegal newspapers, evacuating Jews, and recruiting and instructing saboteurs. Niels knew there was enough evidence to condemn him. He could guess the sentence: death by a firing squad.

CHAPTER TWENTY-SIX

"It struck me that I had made yet another bad mistake by not attempting a break, however desperate. Suddenly the chances I had rated so low seemed quite promising. Bolting through a fourth-floor window or jumping twenty feet to a railroad track while dodging bullets has some merit after all—at least compared with being taken out, reduced to an undignified and futile struggle when being tied to a stake, and shot."

At night, still in the solitary confinement of his small cell, Niels tried to face his fears and be philosophical about dying young. "What then was death to be like? Oblivion, probably, that was nothing to look forward to, but nothing to be afraid of either. Yet, I had to admit to a feeling of fear, the kind we harbor, probably instinctually, toward the unknown. . . .

"My decision four years earlier to fight the Germans had been immediate and spontaneous, voluntarily made, my own initiative. I had wanted active involvement, and I got it. Would history now assign me a role of an unknown martyr, taken from his prison cell to be summarily liquidated, mourned by a few family friends, then forgotten?"

IN THE "HOTEL VESTRE": JØRGEN KIELER

> I am now being held in the German section of Vestre Fængsel and am receiving fair treatment. What the future will bring, I cannot tell. I have no worries in that direction. When you are at peace with yourself, the outside world cannot upset you.
>
> —Jørgen Kieler, letter to his mother,
> February 14, 1944

Like Niels Skov, Jørgen Kieler felt it was only a matter of time before he received the death sentence. His main goal during interrogation was to spare others. His tactics were as follows: "play for time, admit to things they have evidence for, but not until it was really necessary, do not confess to the guilt of others, unless the person concerned was known to be safely in Sweden."

Jørgen also hoped to be recognized as the leader of HD2, to help lessen the interrogations suffered by others and reduce the risk to friends still at large. The young man shouldered his responsibility with full knowledge of what it might mean. "There was no great sacrifice involved in taking on the role of scapegoat. Whether I was condemned to death for one or more acts of sabotage made very little difference. But I hoped that the Germans would be satisfied with one death sentence."

CHAPTER TWENTY-SEVEN

Elsebet Kieler shared her brother's concerns about not telling the Germans anything. She wrote in her prison diary, "'I was very afraid of revealing anything about other people that could do them harm. The constant threat I was under from the Gestapo was that if I did not tell them things, perhaps Mother and Lida would also be arrested. . . .

"'One thing that helped me colossally was when Jørgen came to visit me unexpectedly. I had caught a glimpse of Flemming on an upper floor when we were both going back after exercise. He looked pale and had grown a beard. But Jørgen suddenly turned up at my cell door along with a German soldier and delivered diet bread to me from the Red Cross. . . . As I sank my teeth into it gratefully, I found that it was hollow. Inside lay a farewell letter from Jørgen. He was counting on a death sentence.'"

Jørgen also got an unexpected surprise in prison. His old friend John (Svend Otto Nielsen), who had been wounded and captured back in December, was still alive. Jørgen had always admired John, a dedicated father and teacher. John told Jørgen that he had often talked with his students about the dangers of dictatorship and the importance of fighting for freedom. Now both John and Jørgen realized they would probably die for their principles.

John was still recovering, and Jørgen asked to be allowed to help with his care by carrying him to the exercise yard. Jørgen was touched by his friend's joy at being able to sit outside on a warm April day. There would not be many more. Toward the end of April, word reached the prisoners that there was more unrest in the streets of Copenhagen. The prisoners knew this was likely to lead to reprisals. They were right. On April 27, 1944, John was executed.

His death had a profound impact on Jørgen. He had treasured the short time the two had shared in prison. The young resistance fighter hoped that he "would be able to live up to his example, should it ever be necessary to do so. For the rest of my life, I have lived with the memories of those thirty-six days, and when, after the war, I had need for serious reflection, solace, moral support or inspiration . . . I have time and time again returned alone to his grave."

On May 20, Jørgen's sister Bente was released from prison. Jørgen was able to smuggle out a letter to his father with her. He hoped Bente could get the note to Dr. Kieler, who was being held at a different prison, called Horserød. Jørgen told his father what he expected to happen when their case went to court.

"'Whether or not we will be executed will depend on the situation in the city and the whole country. I am an optimist in these matters, and I ask you to be, too. Should things go wrong, we will have to take it like men, in the knowledge that we are dying for a just cause.

"'Elsebet and Flemming are keeping a stiff upper lip. But the many executions do put a certain strain on the atmosphere in here. . . . We live in a little world, surrounded by bars and grilles. But life is large here too. You just have to live your life as a human being, shut everything else out. You

"John" Svend Otto Nielsen.

see your friends as a shining example, a light that will suddenly be extinguished by ten bullets. But then a miracle happens. The light fades, but a glow remains in our eyes. . . . I promise you that whatever the future may hold, I will accept it with my head held high. Our cause can never die.' "

People run away as a Danish storefront burns in June 1944.

BETWEEN HOPE
AND DESPAIR

In a way, Jørgen Kieler would be glad for it to be over. The "endless demands made during interrogation, the endless swings between hope and despair and the weight of responsibility for the lives of others were taking their toll. I hoped it would all end soon. But it did not."

He was supposed to be sentenced on June 28, 1944; then he was told he would get the verdict on July 5. He had no reason to think he would escape the death sentence—in recent days more executions of saboteurs had taken place. All he could do was wait.

Jørgen woke on Saturday, July 1, to unexpected changes in prison routine. He wrote in his diary: "'There is no gas, light or water in the prison. . . . There is very little food. So the rumors of a strike must be true. . . . The warders are growing nervous.'"

In fact, outside the walls of Vestre Fœngsel prison, Copenhagen was under siege. The news of the successful Allied landing in France on June 6, 1944, had brought expectations of a quick end to German occupation.

American general Dwight D. Eisenhower had given hope to the citizens of occupied countries like Denmark, declaring on the BBC: "'The hour of your liberation is approaching.'" The illegal publication *Frit Danmark*, which the Kielers and their friends had helped produce, responded with enthusiasm: "'We know that it is more than a hope that is being expressed—it is a pledge that we can depend on.'"

A barricade constructed during the 1944 strike.

Sabotage groups increased their activity. In retaliation, Werner Best ordered more executions of activists. On June 25, 1944, in response to unrest in Copenhagen, Best imposed an 8:00 p.m. curfew. One illegal paper noted: "'If Mr. Best thinks the Danish workers without a murmur are going to work for the Germans 8–10 hours and then let themselves be locked up at 8 p.m. in the scorching heat, he has another thing coming.'"

That threat of defiance proved true. Strikes spread; people took to the streets of the city at night, ignoring the curfew altogether and setting bonfires. The city of Copenhagen shut down: There were no transportation or telephone systems. To punish people, Best ordered utilities turned off. Hundreds of bonfires blazed; rioters looted and attacked businesses of pro-German Danes. Trucks carrying German soldiers roared in to keep order but were stopped by homemade barricades. During the last week of June and first few days of July, more than seven hundred people were killed or wounded in what became known as the Copenhagen People's Strike.

Best was in trouble with his bosses back in Berlin once again. He was criticized for executing resistance activists, which was viewed by the Nazis as a practice that helped to create martyrs and fuel turmoil on the streets. Instead, he was told that he should be following "'Hitler's instruction to combat sabotage by terror alone and not by trials in the courts.'"

To restore order, Best was forced to change tactics. Rather than cracking down on the population, he began to negotiate solutions with the Danish Freedom Council, the coordinating body made up of resistance leaders that had formed in

Danish shipyard workers go on strike when prisoners are to be transported via ship from Elsinore Harbor in August 1944.

September 1943. Utilities were turned on, soldiers backed off, and a few days later workers returned to work.

On July 5, the day he thought he would learn his fate, Jørgen wrote in his diary: " 'They have not come to fetch us. Why not?' "

Two days later he got the news. He would not be executed. He concluded: " 'The strike has saved us.' "

...

During those tumultuous last days of June, Niels Skov was also awaiting sentencing. On Saturday, July 1, he realized no water was flowing from the faucet in the small sink in his cell. He got no food that day either. "In my solitary confinement, however,

A woman and two men were shot and killed by German soldiers in the middle of a Copenhagen street during the strike of 1944.

I was blithely ignorant about the reasons. Obviously, something important must have happened."

Soon after, though, the prison routine returned to normal. And still Niels heard nothing about his case. "As week after dreary week went by, even the expectation of imminent death began to lose its dread and was replaced by the calmness of resignation. The Danish summer of '44 was dry, sunny and lovely. In the tiny flower bed visible from my cell window grew one single rose, and when I chinned myself to window height twenty times every morning, I glimpsed its progress from bud to blood-red, magnificent bloom."

Niels passed the time another way as well. His mother had come to visit, bringing cheese, meatballs, and fresh strawberries. "She also brought a piece of needlework canvas and some yarn. She had been told by some that prisoners were being tortured around the clock and by others that we were bored. She preferred to believe the latter and consequently thought the needlework would be in order.

"My time should have run out, and here I was doing embroidery with my hands chained," Niels reflected.

It was a forest scene with an elk, about two thirds of a square foot large.

It seems like something incredibly difficult to do. But, as Niels said, looking at his handiwork seventy years later, "It's not nearly as hard as it sounds when you have unlimited time."

When it was nearly done, Niels sewed his name and date in the corner, then surveyed his accomplishment. "The elk looked impressive, I thought, standing proudly by a forest

Needlepoint that Niels Skov stitched while imprisoned at the "Hotel Vestre."

stream, bellowing a mating call, no doubt. I wondered if I would ever see an elk in the wild."

...

Then, finally, something happened. Said Niels Skov: "One morning in late August, four SS guards had walked into my cell. I half expected to be carted off for execution, but instead they had sullenly removed my chain and ordered me to line up outside together with some two dozen others.

"We were put into two military trucks and under heavy guard rumbled out of town. . . . We were beginning to think ourselves on the way to Germany, but the trip ended just north of that fateful line in the village of Frøslev, where we drove through a gate in a barbed wire fence and were finally told to get off."

This, he realized, was Frøslev, an internment camp in southern Denmark. Niels was relieved to find he knew someone there: His old friend Thies (Carlo Marqvard Thomsen) appeared beside the truck and began pounding him on the back as soon as his feet hit the ground, saying, "'So, they finally brought the hard core down here!'"

Niels found the conditions in Frøslev camp were more tolerable. But Niels and Thies chafed at being locked up. The war was still going on; they couldn't do much to help from inside prison.

One afternoon, as Niels and Thies were debating whether to make an escape attempt, they heard machine-gun fire. A tower guard had shot a prisoner for straying too close to the barbed wire fence. That random killing made up their minds. "We decided to make a break for freedom."

• • •

Jørgen Kieler was also transferred to Frøslev camp. It happened on August 24, the day after his twenty-fifth birthday. While his sister Bente had been released, the Kieler family was well represented in the camp: Elsebet, Jørgen, and Flemming were all there, and their father, Dr. Ernst Kieler, had recently been transferred to Frøslev as well.

The worst thing about Frøslev, Jørgen thought, was "the uncertainty as to what would happen next. At any time at all, we could be sent back to Vestre Fængsel, be interrogated again and even sentenced to death, or could be sent southwards to an uncertain future in a German prison or concentration camp."

Jørgen's brother, Flemming, felt relieved at the looser conditions, writing in a censored letter to home, "'We greeted Father, and now sleep in the same hut and help him with medical matters. You can imagine what it must feel like to be able to mix with everyone and talk to them; this is a big change. The food is also better here. From a small rise in the camp, you can see a hilly area covered with heather, ringed by a forest of firs. It's nicer here than I thought it would be.'"

Jørgen was also glad to be reunited with his father. Dr. Kieler served as the informal camp doctor and was affectionately called Uncle Kieler. Jørgen was surprised by his father's emergence as a popular leader of his fellow prisoners—and a source of information.

"I had known my father as a friendly, smiling and charming man, who, at the same time, was terribly shy," said Jørgen. "Now [that] I met him in captivity I found that he had a whole crowd of friends, who, more than most of the other prisoners, had their finger on the pulse of the camp. . . . My father was the camp news service."

Dr. Kieler had somehow managed to secure a radio, which was hidden under the floor of the room that served as the doctor's office. Going to the doctor was a way not just to get medical advice but also to keep up with the war news and the progress of the Allies.

All went well until September 8, when the camp commandant found the radio set. Dr. Kieler was taken away for questioning, and everyone in camp worried. Luckily he was brought back unharmed.

• • •

One September day a guard came and told Niels Skov his brother and sister had come to visit him. He exchanged a glance with Thies. Both knew that Niels had no brother. In the office, he found two resistance friends, called Hanne and Torben. Using fake IDs, they had used cigars to bribe their way in for a visit. The audacity of their action took Niels's breath away. It also gave him hope.

After fifteen minutes, when the guard signaled the visit must end, Hanne gave Niels a hug and whispered, with her lips close to his ear, " 'Day after tomorrow at two a.m. we'll be outside the fence between second and third guard towers.' "

Thies and Niels set to work to put the plan in place: They would attempt to short-circuit the lights and make their escape.

• • •

The next morning was September 15, 1944. All camp prisoners were woken in the middle of the night and told to assemble in the yard for roll call. From the group, about two hundred people were selected and told to pack their things, while everyone else was sent back to bed.

The group included Jørgen Kieler, his brother, Flemming, their friend Klaus Rønholt (who had been wounded in the last HD2 action), and two other members of HD2. Jørgen was relieved that Elsebet and his father hadn't been selected. (His sister and father were later released.) Jørgen did recognize the car mechanic, Peter Koch, who'd been involved in their last failed sabotage attempt, as well as Laura Lund, his landlady who'd been wounded the day Peer Borup had been killed. As to what would happen next, no one knew. "We did not know if we were going to be executed or deported," said Jørgen.

The group of 196 men and three women also included Niels Skov and his friend Thies. Their chance to escape had vanished.

"At seven o'clock we marched out of the camp to a number of trucks that took us over the border to a small country railway station . . . where we were ordered to get into cattle wagons, forty per wagon. At eleven o'clock in the morning, the doors of the wagons were locked and the train set in motion," Jørgen remembered.

"The time had come for us to pay the price for remaining alive thus far."

The Danish Industry Syndicate in Copenhagen on fire after sabotage in 1944.

You enter a room or a corridor and are told to stand with your face against a wall. Don't stand there in a panic thinking about death. If you're afraid to die it means that you aren't old enough to take part in the struggle for freedom.

—Kim Malthe-Bruun, January 13, 1945

In the midst of this small but utterly evil world where human beings were slowly being reduced to hunted animals, he emanated a strange restfulness, which was marked by both humility and pride. . . . They had tried to remove his right to be a human being, to love humanity, and they had lost.

—Jørgen Kieler, speech given in 1947 at a ceremony to bury Danish concentration camp victims whose remains were brought home. Written in memory of fellow resistance fighter Jørgen Staffeld, who died on Christmas Day, 1944.

deport (v): to carry away, carry off, remove, transport; especially to remove into exile, to banish.

CHAPTER TWENTY-NINE
SEPTEMBER 1944: NEUENGAMME

For two days, Niels Skov had been crammed into a locked freight car with other Danish prisoners bound for Germany. They had nothing to eat or drink. "One never becomes used to being hungry," he said. "Never, never, never."

Niels also never would forget the moment he passed through the gate in the electric fence at Neuengamme, a German concentration camp near Hamburg, Germany. Hope drained away. "We walked to one of the low, ugly buildings where we were ordered to undress for showering. Our clothes went into a large barrel while personal belongings, money and wristwatches went into a smaller one."

The prisoners had their hair shaved. "There is something strange, alienating and demeaning in being shorn of one's hair." It was, Niels reflected, "the first step in a process of methodical dehumanization, of converting us from ordinary healthy citizens into creatures merely caricatures of humanity."

First they were marked as political prisoners by red triangles sewn onto their rag coats, then they were led to wooden barracks. Niels could see what starvation and illness had done to other prisoners, who resembled walking skeletons. "Thies and I realized that we were . . . seeing what we were destined to become sometime in the not too distant future, unless we got out or the war ended. . . . The intent was for us to succumb to illness, hunger or summary execution, whereupon we would disappear into some unmarked grave or otherwise be disposed of as just so much rubbish. In effect, we had been consigned to oblivion."

• • •

Neuengamme had been set up in 1938. Of the more than one hundred thousand people at the camp between 1938 and 1945, it's estimated that more than fifty-five thousand prisoners died. Neuengamme was also used as an outsourcing camp, sending out prisoners to perform hard labor at other subcamps supporting the German war-machine effort.

Saboteurs were not the only Danes sent to Neuengamme. German officials in Denmark had become increasingly displeased with the lack of cooperation from the Danish police in combating resistance and sabotage. They decided to disband the force. On September 19, 1944, more than two thousand Danish police officers were arrested and deported to concentration camps. The captured police officers were sent first to Neuengamme, and from there to Buchenwald camp, where more than fifty perished. The remaining officers were scattered to various work camps in Germany. Back in Denmark, about seven thousand police officers went underground to escape being arrested, and many became active in the resistance movement.

• • •

"It is difficult to describe a concentration camp," Niels Skov said. "The physical conditions can be readily related: the double fences of electrified, barbed wire, the squalid barracks separated by internal fences of barbed wire, the filth, the tiny

Niels Skov (left) and Thies (right).

CHAPTER TWENTY-NINE

ration of low-grade food. What cannot be communicated is the atmosphere, the mood of the place, the pervasive fear generated by the imminence of gruesome death. . . .

"The one and only daily meal was dished out in late afternoon and consisted of a chunk of bread, heavily laced with sawdust, and a bowl of 'soup,' actually salty water with pieces of boiled turnip."

Nothing in his life had prepared Niels for the absolute brutality he now faced. On his second day in camp, he and the other prisoners were forced to watch a Polish woman hanged for stealing a piece of bread, with her baby strung up beside her in a bag. The prisoners endured long hours of standing outside in the dirt, which soon became a "filthy muck" with the rains of autumn.

Each evening, they were made to stand and be counted and recounted, usually in the rain. There was no rest. They were awoken frequently at night and taken to large air-raid shelters. It wasn't to protect them against Allied bombs, Niels realized, but to deprive them of sleep. Worst of all were the inspections by guards, who would walk slowly down the row just waiting for the slightest excuse to single someone out for punishment.

Niels and Thies had managed to get bunks together and made a solemn promise to each other to make themselves a "unit of two." It could, they realized, save their lives. "By sticking together and looking out for each other as we had been used to doing as saboteurs, the two of us would stand a far better chance of coping than one man alone."

Even with all that they had suffered since being arrested,

they now began to understand for the first time the full extent of the Nazi horror. It helped them appreciate as never before what they'd been fighting for back home in Denmark. Reflected Niels: "We never before had come close to realizing the merit of our cause."

In those first days in the camp, Niels and Thies tried to keep their spirits up by talking about their favorite subject: food. Even though they were always hungry, the two young men liked to plan future meals with family and friends in elaborate detail. Niels said, "It's a miracle that our digestive juices did not eat right through our stomach walls."

● ● ●

Like Niels Skov, Jørgen Kieler felt lucky to have someone he could depend on. He and his brother, Flemming, were committed to looking out for each other. Just two days after their arrival, the brothers learned they were being sent to another camp called Porta Westphalica (sometimes spelled Westfalica). "Flemming and I were glad to be among those chosen to go there. It could not get any worse than Neuengamme—at least that is what we thought."

About two hundred prisoners, including ninety-eight Danes, all resistance activists, were assembled for the transport. Said Jørgen: "We went off . . . little knowing that this would cost just under half of us our lives."

THE MINES OF PORTA

Forty-two hours. That's how long Jørgen and Flemming Kieler and other prisoners were packed into cattle cars, fifty men to a car, on the train to Porta. "This was the worst trip I have ever taken in my whole life. . . . We were ordered to sit on the floor with our legs wide apart so that the first row would sit between the legs of the next, as on a toboggan. We were ordered to neither talk nor move. . . .

"The position in which we had been forced to sit became unbearable. But at the slightest attempt to move we were threatened with submachine guns or given a crack of the whip. . . . Our muscles and joints ached terribly, we got bloody rims on our backsides and thighs, and our feet went to sleep. The tightly packed wagon was claustrophobic. . . . The only relief we got was by thinking about how the German railway network was on the point of collapse on account of the bombing raids by the Allies."

The next day, the prisoners convinced one of the guards to allow them the privilege of being able to stand up, one at a time, to stretch their legs. At last they arrived, exhausted, on September 20, 1944. Rumors had circulated that conditions might be better since the camp was in a hotel, the Hotel Kaiserhof, an attractive wooden building set against the hillside. In fact, the prisoners were held behind the hotel in a large unheated hall, its windows blacked out and covered with barbed wire.

"One side of the hall had blocks of bunks, stacked up vertically in fours and in rows of two. The bunks normally had a straw mattress and two thin blankets," Jørgen remembered. "The prisoners were not given a fixed sleeping place and as there were not enough bunks for everyone, there was a daily scramble for a place to sleep and for blankets as two or three men ended up sleeping in the same bunk with or without blankets."

Any remaining hopes that life at Porta would bear the slightest resemblance to a civilized hotel were dashed when Jørgen saw the rope hanging from a ceiling block in the center of the hall. Here was a grim reminder that anyone who tried to escape would be hanged.

When Jørgen arrived, he saw about three or four hundred other prisoners, all trying to get some sleep. This, he soon learned, was the night shift; at the end of the day other men returned to the hall, which was soon bursting with men desperate to get hold of a bowl of terrible-tasting turnip soup and rye bread that served as supper.

The roll call after the meager meal lasted an hour, and Jørgen and Flemming managed to find a bunk to share with two dirty blankets. "We were completely exhausted and soon fell asleep not really knowing where we were and in despair as to what had befallen us."

The day began at four thirty in the morning. Prisoners scrambled to get in line for breakfast: a chunk of bread with a bit of margarine on it and a bowl with something that passed for coffee or tea. They lined up for the three-mile march to a mine called Weser Stolle, where they worked building tunnels

CHAPTER THIRTY

and clearing rubble from underground caverns. The workday lasted twelve hours, followed by the long march back to the cold, grim hall. After another long roll call, which might last an hour or even two, the exhausted prisoners would fall into bed for six hours, until they were awoken again before dawn.

Jørgen tried to keep his spirits up by focusing on the future and what he had heard about the progress of the war. Thanks to his father's secret radio, he knew the Allies had liberated Paris from German occupation on August 25, 1944. It had to be just a short while before Germany would capitulate and the war would be over. "But time dragged on, and despair became evident. I could divide my fellow prisoners into three sorts: optimists, realists and pessimists. Although I realized that our chances of survival were small, I told myself I was an incredible optimist: 'You'll see, you'll make it.'"

Jørgen had to admit that the realists and pessimists were probably closer to the truth of what was likely to happen to them all. The realists figured that even if the war lasted another six months, many of the prisoners would be dead by then. The pessimists agreed with that, and went further—those who did survive would be shot by the Nazis before the camps could be liberated.

Still, Jørgen determined to keep up what he called his "little campaign of hope." He also realized how critical it was for the Danish prisoners to stick together. He was grateful to have Flemming beside him, to help keep an eye on the guards, find a bunk at night, and talk to at the end of the day. "We owe one another our lives."

As a medical student, Jørgen was well aware of the dangers he and the other prisoners faced from the unbearably harsh conditions and poor diet. He was often asked for advice by others about their symptoms. There was little he could do to help.

The conditions at Porta were horrific. Jørgen estimated that he and his fellow prisoners were getting only about six hundred calories a day, not nearly enough to work twelve hours in the mines in freezing conditions, to say nothing of being forced to stand several hours a day for roll calls. There was a severe lack of protein. Weight loss was dramatic, chronic diarrhea common. The men were plagued by flea and lice bites. Starvation, poor hygiene, and infections were the main causes of death.

"As our muscles shrank, an enormous weariness would overtake us . . . which meant that movements became sluggish, and we walked with a stoop and dragged our feet. The extremely starved and permanently freezing prisoners looked like living human skeletons," Jørgen wrote.

At the end of November, Jørgen was assigned to serve in the infirmary. There were no medical supplies or disinfectants, and paper had to make do for bandages. The best the prisoners who served as the staff could do was simply to give patients a rest from work or put them on lighter duty, such as peeling potatoes.

As winter approached, Jørgen felt whatever hope he had kept alive fading. At Christmas the men were given a day and a half off. Some Red Cross parcels that managed to reach

CHAPTER THIRTY

the Danish prisoners were shared, and the men sang carols in Danish, French, and Polish. It was hard to reconcile reality with their memories of past Christmases with loved ones far away.

Jørgen and Flemming went out into the yard. "It was a sharp frost and not a cloud in the sky." Gazing up at the stars, they thought with longing of friends and family back home. "But the cold soon brought us back to Porta and we . . . asked ourselves the eternal question: 'when will this all end?'"

HUSUM

Niels Skov and Thies were kept at Neuengamme for about two weeks before they were sent to a different work camp. Along with other Danish prisoners, they traveled by freight cars north to the port town of Husum, less than fifty miles from Denmark's border.

At Husum, the prisoners were formed into a human chain to unload red bricks from a ship. As he and the others were led through town, Niels couldn't help feeling excited at seeing "real, ordinary people" again. But he was sobered by the townspeople's reaction to the bedraggled prisoners—or rather lack of it. People ignored them. Niels couldn't imagine this same thing happening in Denmark. He felt sure his own countrymen would at least give them a sympathetic glance or a kind word.

While working in Husum, the prisoners lived in a small camp with nine barracks and four toilet sheds, which were really just roofs over open ditches with a pole to serve as a toilet seat. There were four guard towers, one in each corner of the fenced area. Niels guessed the camp had originally been designed to hold about four hundred prisoners. Now it held more than four times that number. In addition to unloading bricks, the prisoners would be digging trenches. This was part of the strategy to defend northern Germany against a possible Allied invasion on the North Sea coast. The prisoners had to attack firmly packed marsh silt with spades and shovels for ten hours a day.

CHAPTER THIRTY-ONE

"Exposure and illness had right away begun to thin our ranks, aided by the grim effects of starvation," said Niels. "To our physical agony was added frustration and anguish from the certain knowledge that our misery and approaching death could be avoided, easily and immediately by something as simple as a bit of food, something we knew to be readily available in our nearby homeland. . . . After a few weeks, our largely liquid diet had begun to cause some serious stomach disorders."

Niels had two bouts with dysentery, growing weaker after each one. The conditions were so crowded, two prisoners were forced to share one bunk. Niels's first bunkmate died in the night. So did the second. The chances of making a break for freedom seemed remote.

"When we returned in the evening and saw the barracks come into view under the slowly ascending smoke from the stoves, the temptation to drop onto a bunk and let sleep—truly the brother of death—bring oblivion was almost irresistible. . . . It was nearly impossible to summon the mental energy to plan a getaway."

Niels felt tormented knowing how close they were to the Danish border. Every day, the landscape reminded him of the beaches of Ribe he knew from his childhood—beaches that were tantalizingly close—only about sixty-five miles away! If only he and Thies could find something to cut through the fence, they might have a chance of reaching Denmark. It was worth a try.

The pile of bricks inside the ship was shrinking. One morning Niels had an idea. He and Thies began to stealthily work their way up along the line of men on the chain, until they were in the hold of the ship itself. Thies kept a lookout on the nearest guard, posted above on deck. Niels stepped to the door of the engine room. A boy who didn't look more than sixteen was working there, a pile of tools beside him.

Niels spotted a pair of pliers with half a jaw broken off. "Throwing caution to the winds, I pointed to the broken pliers and asked him quietly if I could have them to repair my shoes.

"Our eyes met. In an instant of silent rapport we both knew that I didn't intend to repair shoes; we also both knew that a word to the SS guard on deck could have caused my being beaten to death, then and there. After a moment, he shrugged and turned back to his work. . . . I snatched the pliers and tucked them into my pocket."

Niels had one grateful thought. " 'Hitler, you failed to get this boy on your side.' "

■ ■ ■

That night Niels Skov and Thies began to put their plan into action. "The rain was slanting in sheets as we crept on our bellies through the cold mud to the camp perimeter between the two guard towers. At the fence I fumbled for a few interminable minutes with the broken pliers, while Thies's voice from the darkness behind me urged me to hurry."

Niels managed to cut through the two lowest strands of barbed wire. Their goal was to short-circuit the searchlights the following night, and then make a break for it through the hole Niels had opened.

Once again, their escape attempt was doomed by bad

timing. Five other prisoners had planned a break the same night, and their efforts to short out the lights raised an alarm. As a result, the guards carefully inspected the entire fence and repaired the hole the Danes had risked their lives to make.

They would not get another chance. The Husum camp was evacuated at the end of November. But, reflected Niels, "not all of us got to leave. When boarding the dirty and bitterly cold railroad cattle cars, we left behind in sixteen rows of unmarked graves three hundred of those who had entered the camp with us two months earlier."

Among the dead was Jørgen Kieler's childhood friend Klaus Rønholt, who had given his all to the resistance. Along with Elsebet Kieler, he had collected money to help rescue the Danish Jews. Klaus had been wounded in HD2's last sabotage attempt and then arrested and held in prison. Klaus died at Husum on November 22, 1944. He was twenty-one years old.

■ ■ ■

During the grueling two-day trip back to Neuengamme, Niels and Thies sat close, pressed side by side, knees tucked up, trying to stay warm. Twice on the first day, an air raid stopped the train.

On the second day, they heard the drone of planes overhead. "Through the cracks around bolted steel doors we saw an unforgettable sight unfold above us. The bombers were very high, striating the deep blue sky with their vapor trails. At the head of each thin white line, a plane could be seen as a tiny silvery point, as formation after formation of aerial might bore down toward Hamburg in what seemed like endless succession.

"It was our first glimpse of Allied fighting power and we thought it was inspiring. Breathtaking. . . . For the moment misery and nagging hunger were forgotten as we grinned at each other in ecstatic joy. We counted more than eight hundred planes; this could not fail to beat the Germans, and we should see their defeat if only we could stay alive long enough!"

The two young Danes spent another two weeks at Neuengamme before being shipped out to another labor camp. This time they were sent south: away from Denmark, away from hope.

"We went across rivers, through cities, over farmland and through forests, then more rivers, cities, farmland, forests. Being used to a small country that one could bike across in a day and a night, we had a sinking feeling, a sensation of being swallowed up in the vastness of unknown enemy territory," Niels reflected. "Even if we escaped the camp for which we were headed, we would now have untold miles of hostile land between us and home."

■ ■ ■

Niels Skov and Thies were sent to Wansleben, a small satellite camp of Buchenwald concentration camp. Wansleben held about fifteen hundred people at any one time. Tunnels and underground chambers were dug to hold machinery, books, and art objects. Late in the war, as Allied and Soviet troops converged on the area, mine laborers were forcibly evacuated to points farther east. Most or all probably died there in the confusion of the final days of the war. (In 1989, the entrances to the Wansleben mines were sealed; today, only rubble is visible on the surface.)

There was not much of an attempt to mark Christmas Eve at Wansleben. In addition to prisoners, the camp included foreign laborers, mostly Polish, who lived in barracks and whose conditions seemed only a little better off than the concentration camp inmates. But though the factory itself was closed on account of Christmas, the prisoners were made to work, hauling bricks from one side of the camp to the other in single file, each man carrying six bricks at a time.

"It was bitterly cold, and Thies and I critically eyed each other as we shivered in the striped uniforms we had been issued, silently assessing what strength and endurance the other had left," Niels wrote of that bleak Christmas Day.

"Thies had lost a great deal of weight. His six-foot frame was just that, a frame, and he bravely dead-panned a comment about being able to walk through a picket fence by turning sideways. Two inches shorter but more heavily built than Thies, I had lost proportionately less, but my dysentery continued to linger, and almost constant diarrhea had made me permanently tired."

To make the work a little easier, the two friends fashioned a sling to loop around their necks to support the bricks. They tried to keep their spirits up, indulging in their favorite pastime: daydreaming out loud about what they would do after the war and what they would have for dinner when they got out.

"Being able to speak our native tongue and to indulge in lighthearted cursing of our jailers worked like a restorative tonic, lifting weeks of depression from our minds. The labor continued until darkness drove us back to the dormitory building, where the daily bread ration was issued. It was exactly the same meager size as usual. Only the change to cold and clammy outdoor work marked the day as different from any other."

A few weeks later, Niels got a late holiday present: a Red Cross parcel. That the parcel had found him here, in a camp with fifteen hundred prisoners but only three men from Denmark, seemed astonishing. Thies had been moved to a different barracks, but a cigarette bribe enabled Niels to arrange a visit with his friend. The two could hardly believe their luck. The parcel contained cigarettes, which could be used for barter. There was also some food that might just help keep them alive a little longer: a pound of cheese, some dark rye bread, oats, and lard.

Even in his desperate physical condition, Thies hadn't lost his sense of humor. "'You know, Niels, we have both been going downhill rapidly toward the point where a man can neither fart nor beat a drum, but if we consume this stuff slowly, it'll give us a new lease on life.'"

Then Thies added wistfully, "'I wonder if a parcel for me is stuck in the mail somewhere.'"

CHAPTER THIRTY-TWO

WINTER 1945: HOPE FADES

For Jørgen Kieler, his brother, Flemming, and the other prisoners at Porta, the New Year did not bring hope. Conditions in early 1945 only got worse. The effects of starvation, combined with hard, unrelenting labor, claimed the lives of more men each day.

After two months of working eighteen-hour days in the infirmary, Jørgen was sent back to the mines, sometimes on the day shift, other times at night. "The work consisted of drilling six to ten feet . . . into the rock with a pneumatic drill, a cavity in which an explosive charge and a fuse were placed. . . . After the explosion had taken place the loosened rocks and stones were shoveled and lifted out onto a dump wagon, which the prisoners would then push out of the mine.

"My own job meant holding the drill with my bare hands during the pre-blasting phase, until it took in the rock face. Cold water ran down my sleeves and I soon became soaked through and freezing. The vibrations of the drill took the skin off my palms, which in no time at all were full of sores."

Jørgen was worried about his brother's condition too. Flemming was coughing often now, and Jørgen suspected that, like many others, he had contracted tuberculosis.

Jørgen's own ability to fight off starvation grew less each day. His new job made everything worse. He was being forced to drag rails up a steep hillside. At times in the distance Jørgen could hear cannon fire, but there was no way to know what was happening with the war itself. The days when they could rely on his father's secret radio to get news were long gone.

What he did know was that something mysterious was being built in the center of the camp yard. Jørgen had his suspicions: "We were convinced that this was going to be a gas chamber in which we would be murdered at the very last minute."

Jørgen had tried to hold on to hope. Now it was slipping away. "We still tried to have conversations—about the past and the future," he said. "But hopes of ever seeing our families again began to fade. The exhaustion increased and our conversations would peter out. We now began to daydream more, but hunger caught up with us all too soon."

Jørgen no longer dreamed of being free or of the food he would eat someday. Even the images he treasured of home were dying away. "The passing of time became an ever vaguer concept and in the end vanished entirely. We were living in an eternity with no beginning or end. . . .

"I do not think that at any point during my captivity in Denmark or Germany had I been so low, had such feelings of hopelessness and despair as the day I discovered that I could no longer see my parents, sisters and friends in my mind's eye."

"*Hic mortui vivunt*," wrote Jørgen later, recalling the Latin proverb.

Here the dead live.

People celebrating the liberation of Denmark, May 5, 1945.

PART FIVE

LIBERATION
SPRING 1945

Today I was taken before the military tribunal and condemned to death. . . . I'm not of importance and will soon be forgotten, but the ideas, the life, the inspiration which filled me will live on. . . . It is up to you, young and old, to create a broad, human ideal which everyone can recognize.

—Kim Malthe-Bruun, April 4, 1945
July 8, 1923–April 6, 1945 (executed)

liberation (n): the action of liberating (especially from confinement or servitude); the condition of being liberated; release.

CHAPTER THIRTY-THREE

THE WHITE BUSES

Like Jørgen Kieler, Mélanie Oppenhejm and those imprisoned with her in Theresienstadt concentration camp were losing hope. They were always cold, always ravenously hungry. Mélanie and her family struggled to survive on less than half a loaf of bread each week, with a little weak soup made from potato peelings. It was not enough.

Twenty-four Danish inmates died between the fall of 1943 and the time when food shipments began to reach the prisoners in late February 1944. During the next fourteen months, another twenty-seven Danes perished. The food parcels helped prevent some deaths, but sickness and extreme hunger continued to take a toll.

All around her, friends from Denmark were suffering and dying. One had diabetes, but there was no medicine to be had. Said Mélanie: "My husband comforted him with the thought that an ambulance from Denmark would soon be on its way to fetch him home. I think he died without realizing how very ill he was."

Years later, Mélanie still struggled to grasp the horror of that time. "Our existence could not really be called life but a mere semblance of life which is impossible to describe to those who have not actually experienced such conditions."

Yet despite everything, there were few suicides. Mélanie wondered what kept people from giving up. "Was it hope? Did fathers and mothers shrink from taking such steps for fear of abandoning the children they had brought into the world? Or was it that people were too drained of strength and will-power to determine their own destiny?"

• • •

By late February 1945, rumors were flying throughout the camp that Germany would be forced to surrender soon. It wasn't clear what that would mean though. Would Theresienstadt be liberated and everyone rescued? Or were the Nazis planning some horrific scheme to erase all evidence of torture and starvation? Through his job at the camp, Mélanie's husband had overheard talk that the Nazis intended to drown the prisoners in the moat that surrounded the camp, which had once been a fortress.

Then, one April day, all Danish prisoners were moved to chambers below the barracks. They had no idea what this might mean. A few days later, they were told to line up. Mélanie remembered vividly what happened next. "And then we saw a Swede, a real live Swede, wearing a Red Cross uniform. . . . It was indescribable. We hardly dared show our joy but we understood that we might at any moment be collected and escorted away."

Even as Mélanie's own hopes rose, she couldn't forget the prisoners from other countries she had come to know. She feared they had little chance of survival and might all be killed before the end of the war. "And yet we were leaving Theresienstadt. There were the white buses awaiting us. We could not believe our eyes."

And then they were led to the white buses.

...

What were the white buses, and how was it that Danish prisoners were released before the end of the war? The story began months before, when Carl Hammerich, a Danish naval officer and resistance fighter married to a Norwegian woman, raised the idea with Danish officials of obtaining the early release of Danish and Norwegian prisoners. Representatives from Denmark's foreign ministry department began direct negotiations with Germany, including SS chief Heinrich Himmler, sometime in the fall of 1944.

The Swedish Red Cross was also involved, especially Count Folke Bernadotte, who served as vice president of the Red Cross in Sweden and was a nephew of the king of Sweden. In February 1945, Bernadotte was able to meet personally with Himmler, thanks to an intermediary named Felix Kersten, Himmler's personal masseur and a man credited with using his personal influence to save many Jews.

On April 9, 1945, exactly five years after the Danish occupation began, Himmler agreed that Danish prisoners could be released and sent to Sweden for the rest of the war. Three days later, "thirty-five white buses, with the Red Cross and the Swedish flag painted on each side, began their four-day journey to Theresienstadt. It was a dangerous journey for the big buses, driving on the German main roads."

On Sunday, April 15, 423 Danish Jews climbed onto the buses (some sources say 425). The group included three babies born in the camp and several women who had married Danish prisoners.

Danish Jews released from Theresienstadt in April 1945 climb aboard the white buses on their way to Sweden.

Rabbi Max Friediger recalled what it was like as they left. " 'The gate was opened—and we were free men. No one said a word. We simply could not utter a sound.' "

* * *

On the way, the buses stopped near the city of Potsdam, which had just been bombed by the Allies. When the buses stopped, the exhausted prisoners piled out to sit on the grass. "For the first time since deportation we were able to relax in a real meadow," recalled Mélanie.

In another town, people came out when the buses stopped and spontaneously invited the prisoners into their homes to rest for a short while. "I could not get over it," said Mélanie. "There were real washbasins and real soap. . . . I

The white buses.

glanced down and saw a clean and polished floor. . . . It was like a fantastic adventure."

Since Germany still occupied Denmark, the agreement stipulated that the prisoners had to be taken to Sweden. But the buses passed through Denmark before being loaded on ferries to Sweden. On the streets of Denmark, thousands of people cheered and waved flags.

Still, it was hard for Mélanie and the others to convey the horror they had experienced. She did not know how to respond to questions about her deathly appearance. She knew it would be impossible to explain what they had suffered. "Where to start and where to finish?"

Mélanie and her family were now safe. She would not forget what had happened and the people she had met. "I have asked myself many times since then whether it was really me who experienced that hell—and if so, how could I ever have come through it?"

CHAPTER THIRTY-FOUR
THE LAST ESCAPE

By April 1945, the war's end seemed days away. A few months before, on January 27, Soviet troops had liberated Auschwitz and Birkenau concentration camps; at the Yalta Conference on February 4, 1945, leaders from the United States, Great Britain, and the Soviet Union met to discuss plans for Europe after the end of hostilities. The firebombing of Dresden, Germany, began on February 13, 1945. The Allies continued to capture significant German targets.

Even so, for Niels Skov and Thies and many others, survival still hung in the balance.

On April 11, 1945, Niels learned through the grapevine that an order had come to the camp: All the prisoners at Wansleben were to be killed, and German personnel should evacuate. There was a glitch, however. Apparently the guards didn't have enough ammunition to carry out the executions. They then ordered the elevator cables on the mine shafts removed.

It wasn't hard for Niels to figure out the reasoning behind that order: "If the elevator cables were removed from the mine shaft we could all be dumped into that ample hole with firm assurance that a one-mile free fall would accomplish the mission."

For whatever reason, it appears the commander was talked out of this plan, and instead he gave the order to evacuate the prisoners. No one knew where they were going or where the battlefront was. Rumors flew: The Russians were on their way from the east; Americans were coming from the west.

On the afternoon of April 12, 1945, Niels and Thies and other prisoners were marched out of camp and made to shuffle along on a country road. "We walked four and five abreast in what one might describe as controlled disorder, the strongest prisoners toward the head, the weaker receding with the column's tail. On each side walked the guards. They had started out with intervals of a dozen yards apart, with a dozen or so clustered at each end. Prisoners too weak to keep up were summarily shot by the tail guards.

"A couple of times, prisoners had broken from the column and run into the darkness, only to be cut down."

Niels and Thies knew they were too weak to overpower a guard. Nor did they want to be shot in the back after all they'd been through. But they knew this was their best—and maybe last—chance for escape.

They devised a dangerous but ingenious plan. They estimated exactly how many steps it took before the guards, catching sight of an escapee, would let loose a burst of machine-gun fire. They would try to outsmart the guards. But they would have to time this death-defying act precisely.

Niels and Thies felt responsible for the only other Danish prisoner with them, a young man they knew as Benjamin. The three walked up close behind the nearest guard, so that the next one back who would see them run would be as far away as possible. And then came the moment.

"When the sky seemed as dark as we could hope for, we took each other by the hand for support, Benjamin in the

CHAPTER THIRTY-FOUR

middle, and started to run, counting: one . . . two . . . three . . . four . . . five . . . six . . . seven . . . eight . . . nine . . . DOWN. Within less than a second of hitting the ground, we heard a Schmeisser cough a short burst and sensed the bullets just overhead."

They waited, not moving, pretending to be dead. The column seemed very, very close. "It seemed to take forever before they all dragged by and we heard the noise fade in the distance. Then we got up, spied the big dipper through a rift in the clouds and began walking in a westerly direction, stumbling in the dark on uneven ground but making across unknown, open countryside. We were free."

CHAPTER THIRTY-FIVE

HOME: JØRGEN KIELER

A few weeks earlier, on March 18, Jørgen and Flemming Kieler received some unexpected news: The Danish prisoners were being sent back to Neuengamme the next day. The prisoners who were left, that is. Of the 225 Danes who had been sent to Porta Westphalica, only 81 were still alive.

There was another surprise the next day. The prisoners sensed a change in the way they were treated on the return train journey. They were given Red Cross parcels before boarding the train and had straw to lie on.

Back in Neuengamme camp, the Danish prisoners were put together with Norwegians in one large building. Jørgen and Flemming met some of their old friends, who were shocked to see their condition. The prisoners from Porta looked even worse than those who had remained in Neuengamme. Jørgen learned that his friend Klaus Rønholt and Peter Koch, the mechanic who had helped with their last sabotage operation, had both died at Husum.

Now, just as they had in Wansleben and Theresienstadt camps, rumors began to fly. "We heard that we were going to be sent to Sweden and began to imagine that we had a chance of survival, even though we feared the whole time that the Germans would change their minds," said Jørgen.

Jørgen was once again pressed into working as a helper alongside trained doctors in an infirmary for the Scandinavian prisoners. Then he began to feel ill himself. "I noticed increased coughing, accompanied by a high temperature, and strong pains on the right side of my chest. . . . It hurt when I breathed. But I continued my work."

Then they received a visitor: Count Folke Bernadotte of the Swedish Red Cross. For the first time, they heard about the release of Danish Jews from Theresienstadt. Bernadotte and others were now engaged in a flurry of last-minute negotiations to release prisoners in Neuengamme. At last, permission was granted, so long as the operation was concluded by April 20.

When word of the deal reached officials back in Copenhagen, action was swift. "By way of the Danish civil air defense force a total of 114 buses were requisitioned from various owners, eight to ten ambulances, ten trucks, five or six private motor cars and five or six motorcycles, which all reached Neuengamme on April 20 painted white and with

The white buses, filled with refugees rescued from concentration camps, drive through the forest of Friedrichsruh, Germany.

a red cross on the roof. Before the day was out, 4,224 Scandinavian prisoners had been rescued."

Jørgen later wrote about that last day, "'On April 20 the infirmary was emptied and Flemming and I could join the last transport home to Denmark. We were not on the same bus, because I had duties to perform right to the end. We put mile after mile of Germany behind us. . . .

"'Fever, coughing, and the pains in my chest had taken my last strength from me. I was exhausted, but my mood became more buoyant when we passed the border at Padborg. The inconceivable had happened: I was seeing Denmark again.'"

When his bus stopped at the Danish border, Jørgen looked out. "'Among the crowd, I could see a woman looking around for someone she knew. . . . It was my mother.'" After hearing the news of the prisoners' release, she had found a way to get to the border, buoyed by her belief that her sons were still alive.

"'I walked as fast as I could to hug her, and whispered in her ear, "Happy Birthday, Mother." It was her fifty-fifth. We were both speechless. When we had recovered a little, she asked, anxiously, "And Flemming?"'" Jørgen assured her that Flemming had survived and was on another bus.

"'That was her best birthday ever and I cannot remember it without being deeply moved at her boundless love for us.'"

Jørgen and Flemming's journey was not quite over. The German forces in Denmark surrendered on May 4, but the brothers were not there to see it. The negotiations to release the prisoners stipulated that they be taken first to Sweden, where they remained in quarantine until mid-May. The brothers

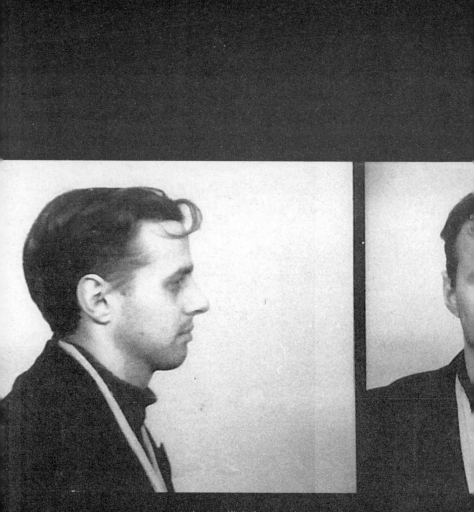
Jørgen Kieler's mug shot.

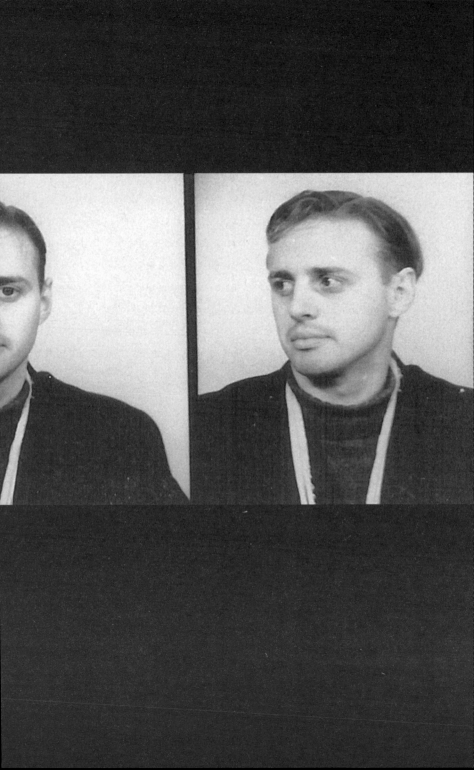

then returned to their parents' home in Horsens and spent the summer recuperating.

All members of the family were now free. It wasn't until he was home with his family that Jørgen truly felt the war was over. Despite four of the five Kieler children and their father being imprisoned for resistance activities, somehow they had all made it. Both Jørgen and Flemming suffered the lingering effects of tuberculosis for years to come. But Jørgen was able to return to Copenhagen in the fall to finish medical school. Subsequently he embarked on a successful career in cancer research. Nor did Jørgen forget the ordeal he had endured: He also conducted research on the effects of hunger on the health of Danish concentration camp inmates and survivors.

"'The miracle had occurred,'" he said. "'The whole family had survived.'"

CHAPTER THIRTY-SIX

HOME: NIELS SKOV

After their daring escape, Niels Skov and his two companions were free men. But they weren't out of danger yet. Far from it. Their striped prisoner uniforms and distinctive shaved heads marked them as prisoners. They couldn't rely on local people to help them. After all, they were in Germany, where young and old were required to turn prisoners in.

Not only that, it was cold. They were poorly clothed, hungry, and weak. Niels summed it up: "We needed to get warm and to rest. Above all, we needed to hide."

The three Danes cautiously approached a farm with a large barn at the edge of a village. A barking dog could be a deadly giveaway. Squeezing inside, they found only a few piles of old, moldy hay, but by lying close they managed to stop shivering uncontrollably. It was, they knew, a precarious freedom. But the Americans must be close. Perhaps their best hope was to lie low and keep watch on the road.

The next morning, their worst fears were nearly realized. As they were moving from one part of the loft to another, the door opened. Perched in the open, they looked down at a soldier who had come inside to clean his machine gun. They stood, unseen, frozen on a plank above his head, trying to hold their emaciated muscles tight, trying not to breathe. Cleaning that machine gun probably took the soldier twenty minutes, Niels guessed, but it felt like a lifetime.

They took turns resting and keeping watch on the road

from a small window in the loft. Suddenly Benjamin whispered, "'Hey, they're coming!'"

Niels spotted a column of six tanks. As one came close to the barn, he recognized it as American. When they hailed the crew, the American sergeant said to his crew, "'Well, lookit them.'" For the first time in his life, Niels was able to practice the English he had studied in school.

The Americans advised the group to head for a nearby town where US military headquarters was being set up. After sharing some rations with the three Danes, they left. Niels and his friends felt more hopeful, but nothing was certain. The situation on the ground was confused and chaotic. Since they were clearly identified as prisoners, they still ran the risk of being shot. Niels decided to opt for a bold approach.

They headed to the largest farmhouse and demanded to speak with the owner. The farmer was not there, but his wife was. Niels informed her that the Americans had appointed him the supervisor of the village, and her farm was to be the headquarters. They toured the farm with her, pretending to be taking notes on conditions for the benefit of what was, in reality, "our imaginative military authorities."

The farm was large, but only four horses and a few cows remained. There were still stockpiles of grain and feed. Niels ordered beds made up for them and, when the woman had gone, the three Danish men burst into laughter. Then they headed straight for the kitchen. Although doctors recommend a special diet for emaciated individuals, they devoured bacon and eggs, bread, cheese, and sausage with no ill effects. After their feast they made cocoa, then heated water on the stove, threw their old clothes in the fire, and took baths. And then they went to sleep in real beds.

The next morning, they decided to head for Eisleben. Niels had two of the horses hitched up to a wagon, and they set off. Once in the town, Benjamin found a truck convoy heading for Paris and decided to go there, hoping to make his way back to Denmark.

In the meantime, Niels encountered a young American officer who didn't speak German. Nor did the local people speak English. Niels stepped forward, offering to help translate English orders into German for the townspeople who would now be under American jurisdiction.

"The American rapidly fired orders right and left. . . . My English held up fairly well, but my school vocabulary had frequent holes," recalled Niels. "We learned that President Roosevelt had died the day before and sensed the momentous importance of losing him, yet hardly turned from what we were doing to contemplate or discuss the event. Among soldiers at war interest vanishes in anything unrelated to the task immediately at hand."

The date was April 13, 1945. The day before, across the Atlantic, President Franklin D. Roosevelt had died of a cerebral hemorrhage, and Harry S. Truman became president. On May 1, they learned that Hitler had committed suicide the previous day. On May 2, at 3:00 p.m., the guns fell silent. Germany surrendered on May 8.

CHAPTER THIRTY-SIX

Niels and Thies were given American uniforms to wear and became unofficial US Army volunteers as part of the effort to collect firearms from people and arrest Nazi officials in the neighboring villages and towns. While still attached to the US military government as an interpreter, work that Niels continued to do off and on until the following year, Thies and Niels obtained permission to return to Denmark for a week to see their families.

Riding in a jeep with an American soldier, they made their way north, taking a ferry to Korsør, a port town on the west coast of Zealand. Once there, Thies was able to call his mother and asked her to let Niels's mother know they were safe.

"Our hearts singing, we streaked across Zealand on an empty highway, every hill and curve familiar and friendly, through Roskilde with its cathedral's green copper spires gleaming in the spring sun, on through the Copenhagen suburbs where flags fluttered from gardens and balconies, and on to the apartment block . . . where my mother lived," remembered Niels.

It had been a long time since that day in April 1940 when Niels had rushed home to see his mother and listen to the news about the occupation on the radio. Now, once again, he was in a hurry.

"I bolted up the stairs, but she was already halfway down to meet me. . . . I was home."

■ ■ ■

Niels Skov.

CHAPTER THIRTY-SIX

Niels Skov would leave that home for the United States a few years later, where he became a successful businessman, then earned a doctorate from Oregon State University before joining the faculty at The Evergreen State College in Olympia in 1972. Given his energy and determination to succeed, it's not surprising that the Niels Skov Scholarship at The Evergreen State College is awarded to students with a passion for entrepreneurship.

Danish children with British and American flags celebrating the war's end, May 1945.

• EPILOGUE •

In those times there was darkness everywhere. In heaven and on earth, all the gates
of compassion seemed to have been closed.
The killer killed and the Jews died and the
outside world adopted an attitude either of
complicity or indifference. Only a few had the
courage to care.

—Elie Wiesel

On May 5, 1945, the SOE's Ralph Hollingworth flew from Great
Britain to Denmark, where he met with resistance fighters to
celebrate a hard-fought victory and stand together on free
Danish soil once more.

Also in those first days of May 1945, a pilot attached to the
Royal Norwegian Air Force in Great Britain was flying near
southern Ireland when he received a call on the radio.

"'"Come back to base immediately."'"

As usual, the pilot had a headstrong response. "'We had
only been flying an hour and a quarter, and it was meant to
be a six-hour patrol, so I replied, "Everything under control, I'm
continuing."

"'But they came back again, even more emphatically:
'"Come back immediately."' That was it, the war was over.'"

Tommy Sneum turned his plane around. After the war, the
former spy would go on to a varied career, one that often
involved his first love: airplanes.

Danish girls on the street holding up newspapers with an announcement of surrender throughout Europe.

There's a story that the broom handle Tommy and Kjeld Pedersen carried in their little Hornet Moth so intrepidly over the North Sea remained mounted on the wall of the air force base near their landing for years to come.

It was just a broom with a ragged bit of cloth attached; yet perhaps it serves as well as anything as a reminder of the courage it took to defy seemingly impossible odds and come through that long darkness into light.

■ ■ ■

Mélanie Oppenhejm and her family were taken to Sweden and kept in quarantine because of the fear of spreading typhoid. She then returned to Denmark, where she continued to work on behalf of refugee children. Many of the children, now with children and grandchildren of their own, gathered to honor her shortly before her death in 1982. Mélanie concluded her short memoir about her survival in Theresienstadt with these words:

"So long as there is even the slightest possibility of the cataclysmic events of history repeating themselves, I feel we have a duty to bring our knowledge of that dark era into the uncompromising light of day. If once one has been trapped in a hell like Theresienstadt, one can never forget it.

"Is it possible that such enormities could ever be perpetuated again?"

■ ■ ■

On October 16, 2014, just a few months before his death at the age of ninety-five, Niels Skov was asked whether he would

British and Danish flags decorate the streets of Copenhagen following the end of World War II and the liberation of Denmark.

have done anything differently. He would do the same things, he affirmed, only he would do them "much better. They would never catch us."

Asked what advice he would give young people today, this forceful, spirited man didn't hesitate. He issued a challenge, advice he himself had followed since that night more than seventy years before, when he had set out to defy a powerful force of evil with a match and a homemade screwdriver:

"Swim against the stream. Don't do what other people do."

• ABOUT DANISH •

Characters of the Danish alphabet and their pronunciations

A a	B b	C c		D d	E e	F f	G g	H h	I i	J j
a	be	se		de	e	œf	ge	hå	i	jåd

K k	L l	M m		N n	O o	P p	Q q	R r	S s	T t
kå	œl	œm		œn	o	pe	ku	œr	œs	te

U u	V v	W w		X x	Y y	Z z	Æ œ	Ø ø	Å å	
u	ve	dobbelt-ve		œks	y	sœt	œ	ø	å	

Omniglot, the Danish online encyclopedia of writing systems and languages, includes a recording of the Danish alphabet: http://www.omniglot.com/writing/danish.htm.

How to Speak Danish: Vowel Sounds

An entertaining video on vowel sounds: http://www.youtube.com/watch?v=1UmFv7T2p68

· PEOPLE IN THIS BOOK ·

Saboteurs

Niels Aage Skov—born November 1919 in Ribe; emigrated to the United States in 1947. He died on January 5, 2015, at the age of ninety-five.

Aage Kjellerup—childhood friend of Niels Skov in Ribe; died in 1995

"Thies" Carlo Marqvard Thomsen (cover name Poul Thiessen)—arrested, May 1944; deported to Germany, September 1944; died in 1985

Student Activists

Jørgen Kieler—born August 23, 1919; involved in illegal newspaper and sabotage group Holger Danske 2 (HD2); arrested, February 1944; deported to Germany, September 1944

Bente Kieler—born September 21, 1920; member of HD2; arrested, February 1944

Elsebet Kieler—born August 4, 1918; member of HD2 who worked to rescue Danish Jews; arrested, February 1944; died in 2006

Flemming Kieler—born June 22, 1922; member of HD2; arrested, February 1944; deported to Germany, September 1944; after the war, became a doctor; died in 2009

Ebba Lund—resistance fighter who organized rescue of many Danish Jews; after the war, became well known for her work in immunology and polio; died in 1999

Klaus Rønholt—HD2 member; arrested, February 1944; deported to Germany, September 1944; died at Husum camp in November 1944

Peer Borup—HD2 member; killed after a failed sabotage attempt in February 1944

"John" Svend Otto Nielsen—helped HD2 as a liaison to the SOE; executed in April 1944

SIS Agents and Colleagues

Thomas Sneum—escaped from Denmark in a Hornet Moth, June 1941; returned as SIS agent, September 1941; escaped to Sweden, March 1942; died in 2007

Sigfred Christophersen—radio operator; parachuted into Denmark, September 1941; escaped, March 1942

Kaj Oxlund—resistance activist; killed in an escape attempt in March 1942

Kjeld Petersen—pilot; escaped in a Hornet Moth, June 1941

SOE Organizers and Agents

Ralph Hollingworth—head of the SOE Danish section, London; died in 1972

Eigel Borch-Johansen (the Duke)—resistance activist; escaped, fall of 1942

Carl Bruhn—first SOE chief organizer; killed while parachuting into Denmark in December 1941

Sir Charles Hambro—head of SOE Scandinavian operations, London

Mogens Hammer—SOE radio operator and resistance organizer; parachuted into Denmark, December 1941; died in 1946

Lorens Arne Duus Hansen—radio operator in Copenhagen

Paul Johannesen—SOE radio operator; parachuted into Denmark, April 1942; killed in September 1942

Ole Lippman—last SOE chief organizer; arrived in Denmark, February 1945

Max Mikkelsen—SOE radio operator; parachuted into Denmark, April 1942

Ebbe Munck—Danish journalist and resistance activist based in Stockholm

Flemming Muus—SOE chief organizer, 1943–1944

Michael Rottbøll—second SOE chief organizer; parachuted into Denmark, April 1942; killed in September 1942

Ronald Turnbull—head of SOE Danish section, Stockholm; died in 2004

Key German Officials in Denmark

Werner Best—German plenipotentiary in Denmark in charge of civilian affairs beginning in 1942; after the war he served time in prison for war crimes; died in 1989

Georg Ferdinand Duckwitz—German attaché reporting to Werner Best; helped to warn the Jewish community; after the war, held government posts for West Germany, including serving for a time as West German ambassador to Denmark; named one of the Righteous Among the Nations, an honor bestowed on non-Jews who risked their lives to save others during the Holocaust, in 1971; died in 1973

Survivors and Helpers

Knud Dyby—police officer who helped rescue Jews; died in California in 2011

Mélanie Oppenhejm—deported to Theresienstadt, October 1943, with her husband and two teenage children; died in 1982

Herbert Pundik—born in 1927 in Copenhagen; escaped to Sweden, 1943; after the war, became a leading journalist

• SELECTED CHRONOLOGY •

1939

September 1
Germany invades Poland.

September 3
World War II begins, as Great Britain and France declare war on Germany.

1940

April 9
Germany invades Denmark and Norway, and the occupation of Denmark begins.

May 10
Germany invades France, Belgium, and Holland.

1941

June 22
Germany violates its nonaggression pact with the Soviet Union and attacks it.

December 7
Japan attacks Pearl Harbor and the United States enters the war.

December 28
The SOE first attempts to drop resistance organizers into Denmark.

1942

January 20
At the Wannsee Conference held in Berlin, senior Nazi officials agree to implement the "Final Solution," which called for sending Jews to camps where they would be murdered.

Summer
Throughout Europe, Jews are deported to concentration camps as part of Nazi plans to exterminate the Jewish population.

November 5
Werner Best arrives in Copenhagen as the German pleni-potentiary of Denmark.

1943

August
Danish workers strike in cities across the country.

August 24
Holger Danske blows up the Forum, a major building in Copenhagen.

August 28
Werner Best gives Danish government an ultimatum.

August 29
Germany declares a state of emergency in Denmark. German general Hermann von Hanneken imposes martial law; King Christian is placed under house arrest.

September 8
Discussions begin between Werner Best and Berlin about removing the Jews in Denmark.

September 28
George Duckwitz spreads warning of German plan to arrest Danish Jews.

October 1
Germans' attempt to round up Danish Jews is mostly foiled, as families go into hiding and escape to Sweden. Danish people help more than seven thousand people to escape.

1944

June 6
D-day—Allied Expeditionary Forces land on France's Normandy beaches.

June 26
Copenhagen People's Strike takes place in late June and early July.

1945

April 15
Danish prisoners are released from Theresienstadt.

April 20
Danish prisoners are released from Neuengamme.

April 30
Adolf Hitler commits suicide.

May 4
German forces in Denmark surrender.

May 7
Germany surrenders, ending the war in Europe.

August 6
United States drops the first atomic bomb on Hiroshima, Japan, and three days later a second atomic bomb on Nagasaki.

August 14
Japan surrenders.

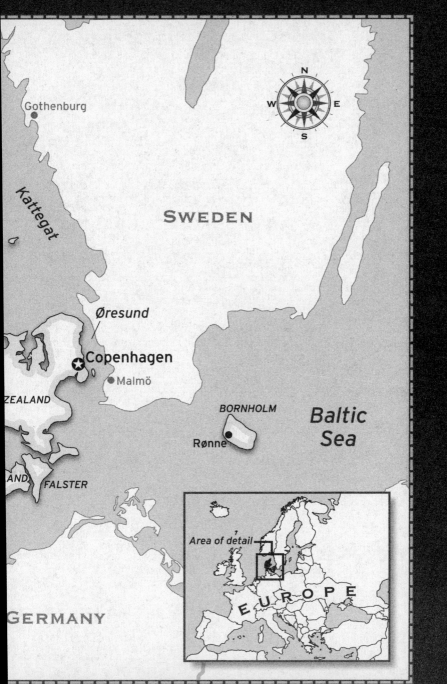

BIBLIOGRAPHY AND OTHER RESOURCES

Selected Bibliography

Ackerman, Peter, and Jack Duvall. *A Force More Powerful: A Century of Nonviolent Conflict*. New York: Palgrave, 2000.

Bak, Sofie Lene. *Nothing to Speak Of: Wartime Experiences of the Danish Jews 1943–1945*. Translated by Virginia Raynolds Laursen. Copenhagen: The Danish Jewish Museum, 2011.

Barford, Jorgen H. *Escape from Nazi Terror*. Copenhagen: Forlaget For Faglitteratur Inc., 1968.

Bennett, Jeremy. *British Broadcasting and the Danish Resistance Movement, 1940–1945: A Study of the Wartime Broadcasts of the BBC Danish Service*. Cambridge, UK: Cambridge University Press, 1966.

Buckser, Andrew. *After the Rescue: Jewish Identity and Community in Contemporary Denmark*. New York: Palgrave Macmillan, 2003.

First International Conference on the History of Resistance Movements. *European Resistance Movements, 1939–1945*. New York: Pergamon Press, 1960.

Flender, Harold. *Rescue in Denmark*. New York: Holocaust Library, 1963.

Gilbert, Martin. *The Righteous: The Unsung Heroes of the Holocaust*. New York: Henry Holt and Company, 2003.

Gill, Anton. *The Journey Back from Hell: An Oral History—Conversations with Concentration Camp Survivors*. New York: William Morrow and Company, Inc., 1988.

Goldberger, Leo, ed. *The Rescue of the Danish Jews: Moral Courage under Stress*. New York and London: New York University Press, 1987.

Greene, Jack, and Alessandro Massignani. *Hitler Strikes North: The Nazi Invasion of Norway and Denmark, 9 April 1940*. London: Frontline Books, 2013.

Gudme, Sten. *Denmark: Hitler's "Model Protectorate."* London: Victor Gollancz Ltd., 1942.

Hæstrup, Jørgen. *Secret Alliance: A Study of the Danish Resistance Movement 1940–45*. Vol. 1. Translated by Alison Borch-Johansen. New York: New York University Press, 1976.

———. *Secret Alliance: A Study of the Danish Resistance Movement 1940–45*. Vol. 2. Translated by Alison Borch-Johansen. Odense: Odense University Press. 1976.

Halter, Marek. *Stories of Deliverance: Speaking with Men and Women Who Rescued Jews from the Holocaust*. Chicago: Carus Publishing Company, 1998.

Hong, Nathaniel. *Sparks of Resistance: The Illegal Press in German Occupied Denmark, April 1940–August 1943*. Odense: Odense University Press, 1996.

———. *Occupied: Denmark's Adaptation and Resistance to German Occupation 1940–1945*. Copenhagen: Frihedsmuseets Venners Forlag, 2012.

Ippisch, Hanneke. *Sky: A True Story of Resistance during World War II*. New York: Simon & Schuster, 1996.

Jespersen, Knud J. V. *No Small Achievement: Special Operations Executive and the Danish Resistance 1940–1945*. Translated by Christopher Wade. Odense: University Press of Southern Denmark, 2002.

Kieler, Jørgen. *Resistance Fighter: A Personal History of the Danish Resistance Movement, 1940–1945*. Translated by Eric Dickens. Jerusalem: Gefen Publishing House, 2007.

Lampe, David. *Hitler's Savage Canary: A History of the Danish Resistance in World War II*. London: Frontline Books, 2010.

Malthe-Bruun, Kim. *Heroic Heart: The Diary and Letters of Kim Malthe-Bruun, 1941–1945*. Edited by Vibeke Malthe-Bruun. Translated by Gerry Bothmer. New York: Seabury Press, 1966.

Manes, Philipp. *As If It Were Life: A WWII Diary from the Theresienstadt Ghetto*. Translated by Janet Foster, Ben Barkow, and Klaus Leist. New York: Palgrave MacMillan, 2009.

Marks, Leo. *Between Silk and Cyanide: A Codemaker's War, 1941–1945*. New York: Free Press, 1998.

Melchior, Marcus. *Darkness over Denmark: A Rabbi Remembers.* London: New English Library, 1973.

Moore, Bob, ed. *Resistance in Western Europe.* Oxford and New York: Berg, 2000.

Nissen, Henrik, ed. *Scandinavia during the Second World War.* Translated by Thomas Munch-Petersen. Minneapolis: University of Minnesota Press, 1983.

Nixon, Edgar B., ed. *Franklin D. Roosevelt and Foreign Affairs.* Vol. II, *March 1934–August 1935.* Cambridge, MA: Belknap Press of Harvard University Press, 1969.

Nytrup, Per. *An Outline of the German Occupation of Denmark 1940–1945.* Translated by Ulrick Norman Madsen. Copenhagen: Danish National Museum, 1968.

Oppenhejm, Mélanie. *Theresienstadt: Survival in Hell.* Translated by Dina Ullendorff. London: Menard Press, 2001.

Paldiel, Mordecai. *Sheltering the Jews: Stories of Holocaust Rescuers.* Minneapolis: Fortress Press, 1996.

Petrow, Richard. *The Bitter Years: The Invasion and Occupation of Denmark and Norway, April 1940–May 1945.* New York: William Morrow and Company, 1974. First Morrow Quill Paperback Edition, 1979.

Poser, Norman S. *Escape: A Jewish Scandinavian Family in the Second World War.* New York: Sareve Press, 2006.

Reilly, Robin. *The Sixth Floor: The Danish Resistance Movement and the RAF Raid on Gestapo Headquarters, March 1945.* London: Cassel & Co., 2002.

Rittner, Carol, and Sondra Myers, eds. *The Courage to Care: Rescuers of Jews during the Holocaust.* New York and London: New York University Press, 1986.

Ryan, Mark. *The Hornet's Sting: The Amazing Untold Story of World War II Spy Thomas Sneum.* New York: Skyhorse Publishing, 2009.

Seaman, Mark, ed. *Special Operations Executive: A New Instrument of War.* London and New York: Routledge, 2006. Published in association with the Imperial War Museum.

Skov, Niels Aage. *Letter to my Descendants*. Odense: Odens
University Press, 1997. (Also available as *Saboteur* from Booklock
.com, Inc., 2007.)

Soumerai, Eve Nussbaum, and Carol D. Schulz. *Daily Life during t*
Holocaust. Westport, CT: Greenwood Press, 1998.

Sutherland, Christine. *Monica: Heroine of the Danish Resistanc*
London: Robin Clark, 1990.

Thomas, John Oram. *The Giant-Killers: The Danish Resistance Movem*
1940–45. New York: Taplinger Publishing Company, 1975.

Tveskov, Peter H. *Conquered, Not Defeated: Growing Up in Denm*
during the German Occupation of World War II. Central Point, (
Hellgate Press, 2003.

Waller, John H. *The Unseen War in Europe: Espionage and Conspir*
in the Second World War. New York: Random House, 1996.

Werner, Emmy E. *A Conspiracy of Decency: The Rescue of*
Danish Jews during World War II. Cambridge, MA: Westview Pr
2002.

Werstein, Irving. *That Denmark Might Live: The Saga of the Dar*
Resistance in World War II. Philadelphia: Macrae Smith Comp
1967.

Yahil, Leni. *The Rescue of the Danish Jewry: Test of a Democr*
Translated by Morris Gradel. Philadelphia: The Jewish Publicat
Society of America, 1969.

Special Interest to Young Readers

Atwood, Kathryn J. *Women Heroes of World War II: 26 Storie*
Espionage, Sabotage, Resistance, and Rescue. Chicago: Chica
Review Press, 2011.

Brinkley, Douglas, ed. *World War II: The Axis Assault, 1939–1942.*
New York Times Living History. New York: Times Books, 2003.

Burgan, Michael. *Refusing to Crumble: The Danish Resistance*
World War II. Mankato, MN: Compass Point Books, 2010.

Byers, Ann. *Rescuing the Danish Jews: A Heroic Story from*
Holocaust. Berkeley Heights, NJ: Enslow Publishers, Inc., 2012.

Levine, Ellen. *Darkness over Denmark: The Danish Resistance and*
Rescue of the Jews. New York: Holiday House, 2000.

Loeffler, Martha. *Boats in the Night: Knud Dyby's Story of Resistance and Rescue*. Blair, NE: Lur Publications, 2000.

Lowry, Lois. *Number the Stars*. Boston: Houghton Mifflin Co., 1989.

Pundik, Herbert. *In Denmark It Could Not Happen: The Flight of the Jews to Sweden in 1943*. Jerusalem: Gefen Publishing House, 1998.

Online Resources: Interviews, Websites, and Museums

There are numerous resources on World War II online. Here are several that may be of special interest in learning more.

June 6, 1944: D-day

http://www.army.mil/d-day/index.html?from=r_l

Danish World War II pilots

http://www.danishww2pilots.dk/profiles.php?id=21

The Frøslev Camp Museum

http://natmus.dk/en/the-froeslev-camp-museum/

Imperial War Museums

http://www.iwm.org.uk/

Jewish Foundation for the Righteous: Jørgen and Elsebet Kieler

http://www.jfr.org/pages/rescuer-support/stories/denmark-/-jorgen -and-elsebet-kieler

The Museum of Danish Resistance

http://natmus.dk/en/the-museum-of-danish-resistance/

Neuengamme Concentration Camp

http://www.kz-gedenkstaette-neuengamme.de/index.php?id=20

Porta Westfalica-Barkhausen

http://www.kz-gedenkstaette-neuengamme.de/index.php?id=3332 &tx_hnlager_pi1%5Buid%5D=126&tx_hnlager_pi1%5BfromPid%5D =952&cHash=c5d722a24482a3ce3fa4f0365ec64353 (Photos and information on the camp where the Kieler brothers were imprisoned)

United States Holocaust Memorial Museum

http://www.ushmm.org/ (Resources include an animated map of the rescue of more than seven thousand Danish Jews: http://www.ushmm.org/wlc/en/media_nm.php?MediaId=3374)

Wansleben

http://ic.galegroup.com/ic/whic/PrimarySourcesDetailsPage/PrimarySourcesDetailsWindow?displayGroupName=PrimarySources&disableHighlighting=false&prodId=WHIC&action=e&windowstate=normal&catId=&documentId=GALE%7CCCX2560000077&mode=view&userGroupName=seat24826&jsid=f4b82543b53bbedc943e5266238e977c

Testimonies and Interviews

Leo Goldberger

Oral history interview with Leo Goldberger: http://www.youtube.com/watch?v=Z87OVlaahjl

Ralph Hollingworth

"Spy Who Outwitted the Nazis." *Market Harborough People*, 26 March 2011. http://www.marketharboroughpeople.co.uk/news/Spy-outwitted-Nazis/story-10877385-detail/story.html

Ebba Lund

Harrison, Donald H. "Girl in Red Cap Saved Hundreds of Jews." Interview with Ebba Lund, January 14, 1994. *San Diego Jewish Press-Heritage.* http://www.jewishsightseeing.com/denmark/copenhagen/1994-01-14_red_cap_girl.htm

Herbert Pundik

"From the Memoirs of Herbert Pundik." *The Righteous Among the Nations.* Retrieved from http://www1.yadvashem.org/yv/en/righteous /stories/related/pundik_memoirs.asp

Oral history interview with Herbert Pundik, United States Holocaust Memorial Museum. http://collections.ushmm.org/search/catalog /irn504561

• SOURCE NOTES •

Every effort has been made to convey source quotations accurately. In some instances, ellipses preceding and following quotations have been removed in accordance with *The Chicago Manual of Style* guidelines.

Epigraph
"This is an extraordinary time . . .": Malthe-Bruun, *Heroic Heart*, 138.

Prologue
Compiled and detailed account: Yahil, *Rescue of Danish Jewry*, 318, 319.
"This remarkable rescue . . .": ibid., x.
"they merely did the . . .": ibid., xii, 393.

Part One
"I feel that I must always . . .": Malthe-Bruun, 138.
Definitions: *Oxford English Dictionary*.

Chapter One
"'Niels, there are foreign soldiers . . .'": Skov, *Letter to my Descendants*, 116.
"I slowed and rode by them . . .": ibid.
"'They say the Germans are rolling . . .'": ibid.
"Riding along . . .": ibid.
"enraged, embarrassed, ashamed.": ibid.
"So this was what . . .": ibid., 117.
"I saw with complete certainty . . .": ibid.
Struggling medical student: For student life in Copenhagen, see Kieler, *Resistance Fighter*, 28–29.
"We heated . . .": ibid., 27.
"We froze,": ibid., 29.
"We got dressed . . .": ibid., 20.
"We felt boundless shame . . .": ibid.
"In 1940, my brother, sisters . . .": ibid., 27.
Danish planes damaged in the invasion: Greene and Massignani, *Hitler Strikes North*, 103. For details of the fall of Denmark, see 88–107.
"drive or march . . .": ibid., 89.
"'I have not the slightest doubt . . .'": ibid., 90.
"a convenient stepping stone.": Hong, *Sparks of Resistance*, 30.
Kurt Himer flew into Copenhagen in advance of the invasion: Greene and Massignani, 98.
"'set in motion . . .'": ibid., 99.
"I will never forget . . .": Rittner and Myers, *Courage to Care*, 90–91
April 9, 1940: For details of events, see Greene and Massignani, 100–104.

Chapter Two
"lay inert and invisible, . . .": Skov, 120.
"primal, defensive instinct": ibid., 118.
"'quiet and restrained demeanor . . .'": ibid., 120.
"Well, they could shove . . .": ibid.

"private war against . . .": ibid., 126.

"attractive and probably easy . . .": ibid., 127.

"It was ten o'clock . . .": ibid., 124.

"With my left hand . . .": ibid., 127.

"The fuel caught . . .": ibid.

"I also realized . . .": ibid., 128.

"There are more matches . . .": ibid., 127–128.

German-Danish relations: First International Conference, *European Resistance Movements,* 150–153.

As resistance historian Jørgen Hæstrup put it, "A free Danish government which . . . could call for resistance and aid resistance was consequently never created. Resistance was never legalized.": ibid.,151.

"The Danish Resistance . . .": ibid., 153.

"Lovely Denmark with forested coasts . . .": Hong, *Sparks of Resistance,* 87.

grassroots resistance: Posters and other resistance tactics in ibid., 96–103. Hong also includes data on the number of cases investigated by the authorities.

At movie theaters: ibid., 112–114.

"'I did not want to arrest . . .'": Loeffler, *Boats in the Night,* 32.

Spitting: Hong, *Sparks of Resistance,* 116, note 4.

"dissidents to official policy . . .": ibid., 115.

Chapter Three

"'They'd never reach us. . . .'": Ryan, *Hornet's Sting,* 17.

"'made me certain . . .'": ibid., 22

"'We need to understand . . .'": ibid., 36.

"'You could use . . .'": ibid.

"'I couldn't believe it. . . .'": ibid., 38.

"'It was one of the most dangerous . . .'": ibid., 39.

"'There's somebody coming.'": ibid., 41.

"'I crouched down . . .'": ibid.

"'Their blind spot . . .'": ibid., 42–43.

"'I had already decided . . .'": ibid., 44.

Chapter Four

Ralph Hollingworth in prewar Copenhagen: Jespersen, *No Small Achievement,* 44.

"'I was to go to London . . .'": Hæstrup, *Secret Alliance,* Vol. 1, 52.

"'Here we were told out'": ibid.

"'to raise a Resistance struggle . . .'": ibid.

"'I had to start absolutely from scratch, . . .'": Hæstrup, Vol. 1, 59.

"an apparently unstoppable": Jespersen, 24.

"foster the spirit . . .": ibid., 509.

Number of SOE agents to Denmark and Norway: ibid., 509–510.

Ebbe Munck's role: ibid., 46–47.

"'Sir Charles was perfectly . . .'": Hæstrup, Vol. 1, 49.

"'I made it clear . . .'": ibid., 50.

"'My orders from Hambro . . .'": ibid., 59.

Chapter Five

"'Sir . . . what would your answer be . . .'": Ryan, 49.

"'Then she's yours.'": ibid.

"'I don't want to hear from you . . .'": ibid., 50.

"'Are they sending a plane?'": ibid., 51.

" 'What? You want to . . .' ": ibid.
" 'Just land in the North Sea . . .' ": ibid.
" 'Little by little, . . .' ": ibid., 67.
" 'Can we make it?' ": ibid., 68.
" 'Of course we'll make it.' ": ibid.
" 'Our only map . . .' ": ibid., 70.
" 'Contact!' ": ibid.
"I had to go down . . .": ibid., 72.
" 'Up! Up!' ": ibid.
" 'They were looking . . .' ": ibid.

Chapter Six
" 'How is she flying?' ": Ryan, 74.
" 'The left wing feels...' ": ibid.
"Puffs of black smoke . . .": ibid., 77.
" 'Up, up!' ": ibid., 78.
"There was an opening . . .": ibid., 81.
"No words will ever convey . . .": ibid.
" 'Find the life jackets,' ": ibid., 82.
"We were both positive . . .": ibid., 83.
"The plane suddenly . . .": ibid.
" 'Don't fall down . . .' ": ibid., 84.
" 'Thanks, Pedersen . . .' ": ibid.
"The wind was howling . . .": ibid., 85.
"I think we were . . .": ibid.
" 'At first I couldn't . . .' ": ibid., 85–86.
"I struggled to bend . . .": ibid., 86.
"Kjeld was spilling . . .": ibid.
"The field came alive . . .": ibid., 91.
"We were just happy . . .": ibid.
"We had fresh . . .": ibid.
" 'Flight Lieutenants . . .' ": ibid., 94.
" 'In that? . . . Not a chance.' ": ibid.

Chapter Seven
"I was aware . . .": Ryan, 102–103.
" 'I went mad . . .' ": ibid., 103.
" 'Do you know . . .' ": ibid.
" 'They . . . couldn't really make out . . .' ": ibid., 104.
" 'Freya radar . . .' ": ibid.
" 'These are the first pictures . . .' ": ibid.,105.
" 'Gentlemen, . . . I think . . .' ": ibid.
" 'the sole relics . . .' ": ibid.
" 'I answered that . . .' ": ibid., 112.

Chapter Eight
" 'Has anyone bothered . . .' ": Skov, 130.
" 'But what can we do?' ": ibid.
" 'As I see it . . .' ": ibid., 130–131.
" 'Are you saying . . .' ": ibid.
" 'No. I think our careers . . .' ": ibid.
" 'Tell me about it.' ": ibid.
"Aage had placed himself . . .": ibid., 132.
"I fumbled, found . . .": ibid., 133.
"Under the tank . . .": ibid.
" 'All quiet?' ": ibid.
" 'Phew, this is going to explode . . .' ": ibid.
"The fuel lit . . .": ibid.

Chapter Nine

" 'I'll do my bit . . .' ": Ryan, 133.

" 'I felt something sharp . . .' ": ibid., 141.

" 'It was excruciating work . . .' ": ibid.

" 'That got me worried. . . .' ": ibid., 142.

" 'I thought . . .' ": ibid., 144.

" 'My heart was pounding . . .' ": ibid.

Hospital: According to Sneum, Professor Chievitz arranged with a colleague and diabetes expert, Dr. Hagedorn, to fake a false-positive diagnosis of diabetes for Sneum should he ever need to get off the street and hide in the hospital. Ryan, 145.

" 'The Princes are . . .' ": Jespersen, 110.

"It had to be a partnership . . .": ibid. Jespersen, along with Hæstrup, provides a detailed chronicle of the SOE's relationship with the Princes throughout the course of the war.

"Even with the best will . . .": Jespersen, 111.

The difficulty in the Danes being able to see the differences in internal British intelligence agencies was noted by Ronald Turnbull in his report to Ralph Hollingworth on December 6, 1941. See Jespersen, 109–111.

" 'I told them . . .' ": Ryan, 150.

" 'Strange weather . . .' ": ibid., 151.

" 'It was because . . .' ": ibid., 184.

"a spy's dream . . .": ibid., 185.

Sneum's radio transmissions: ibid., 208–209.

Thomas Sneum was in contact with Niels Bohr, a Danish physicist.: ibid., 207.

" '. . . I was afraid . . .' ": ibid., 182.

Chapter Ten

"Where is my bag? . . .": Hæstrup, Vol. 1, 88.

BOOKLET: Jespersen, 80–81.

" 'a fine man, . . .' ": Hæstrup, Vol. 1, 81.

"Bruhn's death . . .": ibid., 88.

" 'When he landed . . .' ": ibid., 89.

Mogens Hammer was most definitely: A reward of 5,000 kroner was offered. Kieler, 37–38.

" 'One fine day . . .' ": Hæstrup, Vol. 1, 91.

Chapter Eleven

" 'Do you have a spare key?' ": Ryan, 203.

" 'You can see the street . . .' ": ibid.

Yet in the end, only Christophersen: Christophersen biography, http://www.danishww2pilots.dk/profiles.php?id=21.

" 'Sneum, you have my word . . .' ": Ryan, 238.

" 'We had tried . . .' ": ibid., 246.

" 'You have to keep moving . . .' " : ibid., 255.

" 'It was like rolling thunder . . .' ": ibid., 257–258.

" 'When the biggest crack . . .' ": ibid., 259.

" 'We thought they were our saviors . . .' ": ibid., 260.

Chapter Twelve

" 'I feel obliged to tell you . . .' ": Ryan, 261.

" 'I got scared when I heard . . .' ": ibid.

Sneum incident: ibid., 277–313.

" 'They were worried . . .' ": ibid., 331.

Chapter Thirteen

"'There are some situations . . .'": Jespersen, 98.

"against German shipping, . . .": ibid., 124.

"'The aircraft arrived . . .'": Hæstrup, Vol. 1, 118.

"'He was burning . . .'": ibid., 128.

"'very frightened of taking part . . .'": ibid., 150.

"'who could get in contact . . .'": ibid., 149.

"All its members . . .": Jespersen, 153.

"'At last I heard . . .'": Hæstrup, Vol. 1, 153.

"'When darkness fell . . .'": ibid.

"'We heard footsteps . . .'": ibid., 153–154.

"'I asked him . . .'": ibid., 158–159.

Chapter Fourteen

"With my eyes adjusted . . .": Skov, 178.

"Matches in hand . . .": ibid.

"'Well . . . one thing I can . . .'": ibid., 179.

BOPA: For a more thorough discussion of BOPA, see Hong, *Occupied*, 120–127.

Churchill Club: Werner, *Conspiracy of Decency*, 20–21.

"This requires the cooperation . . .": Hong, *Sparks of Resistance*, 187.

"'Action is required . . .'": Bennett, *British Broadcasting*, 80.

Chapter Fifteen

"I had no idea . . .": Kieler, 40.

"daily moral pressure . . .": ibid., 45.

Infiltration of the *De Frie Danske* group: Hong, *Sparks of Resistance*, 189.

"'would attract attention . . .'": ibid., 190.

"'Do not think . . .'": ibid., 192.

Freedom Council: The SOE's Flemming Muus became an observer at meetings. Hong, *Occupied*, 215–216.

"with great emotion . . .": Kieler, 45–46.

"We could wait no longer. . . .": ibid.

Producing *Frit Danmark*: ibid., 53. Hong's *Sparks of Resistance* includes detailed information on production and distribution of illegal publications.

"banging away . . .": Kieler, 53.

"typed away . . .": ibid.

"We would write . . .": ibid.

For information on illegal publications, see First International Conference, *European Resistance Movements*, 153–154.

"'a born organizer . . .'": Hæstrup, Vol. 1, 179.

Success of Flemning Muus: ibid., *I* 209–210.

Data on supply drop: Hong, *Occupied*, 157–159. One hundred containers were dropped in 1943 compared to none the previous year.

Four thousand containers: ibid., 159.

"'We seem to have been piling . . .'": Jespersen, 169.

Flemming Muus: ibid., 378–379.

"'the call to sabotage . . .'": Hæstrup, Vol. 1, 173.

"Could I be encouraging others . . . ?": Kieler, 57.

"Denmark's ever-increasing . . .": ibid., 59.

Chapter Sixteen

"Once I had decided . . .": Kieler, 60.

"The first was a lack of explosives . . .": ibid., 61.

"We cycled very carefully . . .": ibid., 62.
"I went to bed immediately . . .": ibid.
"We had started from scratch . . .": Kieler, 64.

Part Two
"Courage is never alone . . .": Rittner and Myers, 149.
"Two of my friends . . .": Malthe-Bruun, 139.
Definitions: *Oxford English Dictionary.*

Chapter Seventeen
It was Sunday . . . : Kieler, 67.
The man who headed: Werner Best took over as plenipoten-
    tiary in November 1942 from Cécil von Renthe-Fink. Pretow,
    The Bitter Years, 198.
"country without major problems.": ibid., 185.
July 6, 1943, and Frikorps Danmark: Hong, *Occupied,* 164–167.
For Danes suffering: ibid., 173.
Sit-down strike in Odense: ibid., 173–175.
" 'a city in open revolt' ": ibid., 175.
Werner Best was summoned: Hæstrup, Vol. 1, 258–259, and
    Hong, *Occupied,* 185.
list of demands: The ultimatum also required that all guns be
    turned in and no public gatherings be held. Petrow, 191.
"Danish police officers . . .": Kieler, 75–76.
"regrets that it cannot . . .": Petrow, 192.
Danish Army and Navy: ibid., 193.
"By the morning of August 29 . . .": ibid., 194.
"AT LAST— . . .": Kieler, 65.

Chapter Eighteen
Where there is room . . . : Yahil, 240.
Jews . . . withdrawn from public life: Hong, *Occupied,* 187–192.
" 'I know what I have to do.' ": Petrow, 201.
He first learned from Best: Interpreting Best's role and complex
    motivations in the roundup of the Danish Jews continues to
    be the subject of debate among historians. See Hong,
    Occupied, 192–208.
" 'If there are any . . .' ": Pundik, *In Denmark,* 12.
" 'We have been warned . . .' ": ibid.
"We knew that, at best . . .": ibid.
"We hardly knew . . .": ibid., 13.
"We were frightened . . .": ibid., 14.
" 'I went from house to house. . . .' ": ibid., 28. From an unpub-
    lished account by Robert Pedersen in the archives of
    Herbert Pundik.
" 'There was light . . .' ": ibid., 30.
" 'We kept on . . .' ": ibid., 29–30.
" 'In a half-choked voice . . .' ": ibid., 30. For accounts of the
    roundup, see Yahil, 168–195, and Hong, *Occupied,* 192–198.
" 'Police vans proceeded . . .' ": Yahil, 184.

Chapter Nineteen
"A printing press mechanic . . .": Skov, 203.
"would stick to me . . .": ibid.
"one short jump . . .": ibid.
" 'The easiest, of course . . .' ": ibid., 206.
"The place could be . . .": ibid.
" 'You know, if we could grab . . .' ": ibid., 207.

"watery avenues.": ibid.
" 'I wonder who . . .' ": ibid.
"I thought, perhaps for the hundredth time, . . .' ": ibid.
"Finishing our beer, . . .": ibid.
"I stood at the iron railing . . .": ibid., 208–209.
"Thies came over . . .": ibid., 209.
"a loose network . . .": ibid., 210.

Chapter Twenty
"general headquarters": Entry from Elsebet Kieler's diary excerpted in Kieler, 58.
"The costs involved . . .": Kieler, 100.
" 'Our various hosts . . .' ": ibid., 97.
" 'You handle the ladies,' . . .": ibid., 97–98.
"Ebba was good at convincing . . .": ibid., 98.
Ebba became so well known: see Kieler, 99. Ebba is also featured in Atwood, *Women*, 158–164.
"Once we had become established . . .": Kieler, 100.
"If there were no complications . . .": ibid., 101.
" 'One day, I remember . . .' ": ibid., 102–103.
" 'Then they turned . . .' ": ibid.
" 'We did as much as we could . . .' ": Loeffler, 32.
" 'Don't you think . . .' ": ibid., 63.
" 'I knew the Gestapo . . .' ": ibid., 64.
" 'Somebody always seemed . . .' ": ibid.
" 'was a poor fisherman . . .' ": ibid., 64–65.
" 'Then I realized . . .' ": ibid., 65–66.
" 'I didn't shave . . .' ": ibid., 66.
" 'in the darkness . . .' ": ibid.
" 'In the night . . .' ": ibid., 66–67.
" 'In the gray morning . . .' ": ibid., 67.
" 'Although I was dressed . . .' ": ibid., 67–68.
" 'I purposely did not . . .' ": ibid., 71–72.
" 'Surely, you felt . . .' ": ibid., 116.
" 'away from the Nazi madmen . . . ' ": ibid.
"We were sitting . . .": Pundik, 43.
"The odds were poor . . .": ibid., 48.
"Nicolaisen found . . .": ibid., 49.
"A Swedish patrol boat . . .": ibid.
7,200 Danish Jews escaped: Yahil, 26.
"a tiny nation . . .": ibid., xi.
" 'Among the Danish . . .' ": ibid., 229–230.
" 'Before I left Copenhagen . . .' ": ibid., 239–240.
" 'In train, . . .' ": ibid., 232.
"The thousands and thousands . . .": Pundik, 167.

Chapter Twenty-One
Drowned while attempting: Bak, *Nothing to Speak Of*, 74.
Numbers deported: Yahil, 291.
" 'We were shown . . .' ": Bak, 88.
" 'One night . . .' ": ibid., 91.
" 'Tonight it is . . .' ": ibid.
"The floorboards were . . .": Oppenhejm, *Theresienstadt*, 21.
"Forty thousand people . . .": ibid., 22–23.
"I well remember, . . .": ibid.
Werner Best, probably for . . . : Best met with Adolf Eichmann on November 2, 1943. See Hong, *Occupied*, 209.
"They would be sent back . . .": Oppenhejm, 48.

a postcard might say . . . : ibid., 45.
"Life for us . . .": ibid., 47–48.
International Red Cross visit to Theresienstadt: See Bak, 97.
"no means of penetrating . . .": Oppenhejm, 65.
" 'The mind was fortified . . .' ": Yahil, 295.

Part Three
"Many times during the past two days . . .": Malthe-Bruun, 140–141.
Definition: *Oxford English Dictionary*.

Chapter Twenty-Two
Holger Danske: Hong, *Occupied*, 259–260.
HD2: Kieler, 123.
"would come to Denmark . . .": ibid.
"was considered a man's job,": ibid., 124.
"were fully aware . . .": ibid.
" 'Our friends marveled . . .' ": ibid., 125.
"We considered this life . . .": ibid.
Erik Jens Peter Petersen: Jespersen, 190, 319, 391.
"Jens Peter did not beat about the bush": Kieler, 124.
sabotage attempt: ibid., 127–128.
"I informed him . . .": ibid., 131.
"I had gone into the struggle . . .": ibid., 133.
"Otherwise I would never . . .": ibid., 134.
"John's arrest . . .": ibid., 150.
"a flying squad,": ibid., 151.
"an aerial bombardment . . .": ibid., 152.
" 'When we had agreed . . .' ": ibid., 153.
"But in reality there were ten,": ibid., 153–154.
"One of the engineers . . .": ibid., 161.
"The B&W operation . . .": ibid., 167.

Chapter Twenty-Three
"But the operation . . .": Kieler, 168.
Peter Koch and Laura Lund: Kieler identifies Koch and Lund by last name only; a Danish Wikipedia article on Peer Borup identifies Peter Koch. See http://da.wikipedia.org/wiki/Peer _Borup. Laura Lund is identified in a book in Danish on the fates of Danish women in Ravensbruck by Anders Otte Stensager.
"We in our group . . .": Kieler, 172.
"I suddenly heard . . .": ibid.
"We had the choice . . .": ibid., 175.

Chapter Twenty-Four
telegram to Koch: Kieler, 176.
"We knew it must be . . .": ibid., 177.
"We had to get away . . .": ibid., 178.
" 'Jørgen, look at my legs!' ": ibid., 179.
" 'No, Jørgen, I can't manage . . .' ": ibid., 179.
"I still remember it . . .": ibid., 180.
"But I had more important . . .": ibid.
" 'Where are the other two?' ": ibid., 181.
"Klaus lay there . . .": ibid., 181–182.
"It was something of a miracle . . .": ibid., 182.
" 'Play for time . . .' ": ibid., 184.
"The saboteurs were all prepared . . .": ibid.

" 'The whole of the town . . . ' ": ibid., 192.
Kieler family situation: ibid., 205–216.
"My family and I . . .": ibid., 205.

Chapter Twenty-Five
"My days had turned into . . .": Skov, 217.
"mysteriously seemed to come . . .": ibid.
"Jørgensen is a common . . .": ibid., 218.
"Then I went to the print shop . . .": ibid., 255.
"Thies would not have told him . . . ": ibid.
"I was shoved into it . . .": ibid.
" 'Well, Aage Jørgensen, . . .' ": ibid., 256.
" 'No, you didn't. . . .' ": ibid.
"We were in the truest sense . . .": ibid.
"Did they have enough on me . . .?": ibid.
"names and details . . .": ibid., 257.
"reached over and slowly . . .": ibid.
" 'Maybe now you would . . .?' ": ibid.
"Two prison guards...": ibid., 258.
"It was a completely new . . .": Author interview with Niels Skov,
     October 16, 2014.
"The coarse blankets . . .": Skov, 258.

Chapter Twenty-Six
D-day: http://www.army.mil/d-day/index.html?from=r_l.
Globus factory: Hong, *Occupied*, 238–240.
"The other branch . . ." : Skov, 259.
"In downtown traffic . . .": ibid., 260.
"Suddenly, there was Thies . . .": ibid., 268.
" 'Well, this . . . guard obviously . . .' ": ibid., 269.
"It struck me . . .": ibid.
"What then was death . . .": ibid., 270.

Chapter Twenty-Seven
I am now being held . . . : Kieler, 207.
"play for time . . .": ibid., 216.
"There was no great sacrifice . . .": ibid., 216.
" 'I was very afraid . . .' ": ibid., 227–228.
"I would be able to . . .": ibid., 225.
" 'Whether or not we will be executed . . .' ": ibid., 234.

Chapter Twenty-Eight
"endless demands . . ." Kieler, 238.
" 'There is no gas,' ": ibid., 239.
" 'The hour of your liberation . . .' ": Hong, *Occupied*, 269.
" 'We know that it is . . .' ": ibid.
" 'If Mr. Best . . .' ": ibid., 271–272.
Copenhagen People's Strike: ibid., 269–285.
" 'Hitler's instruction . . .' ": Kieler, 243.
" 'They have not come . . .' ": ibid., 241.
"In my solitary confinement . . .": Skov, 275.
"As week after dreary week . . ." ibid., 275–276.
"She also brought . . .": ibid., 273–274.
"My time should have run out . . .": ibid., 273.
"It's not nearly as hard . . .": Author interview with Niels Skov,
     October 16, 2014.
"The elk looked impressive . . .": Skov, 277.
"One morning in late August . . .": ibid., 280.

" 'So, they finally brought . . .' ": ibid., 281.
conditions in Frøslev camp: ibid., 283.
"We decided to make . . .": ibid., 284.
"the uncertainty as to what . . .": Kieler, 243.
" 'We greeted Father . . .' ": ibid., 244–245.
"I had known my father . . .": ibid., 245. See also Elsebet Kieler's
    letter, Kieler, 244.
" 'Day after tomorrow . . .' ": Skov, 284.
"We did not know . . .": ibid., 246.
196 men and three women: ibid., 252.
"At seven o'clock we marched . . .": ibid., 247.

Part Four
"You enter a room . . .": Malthe-Bruun, 144.
Definition: *Oxford English Dictionary*.

Chapter Twenty-Nine
"One never becomes . . .": Skov, 287.
"We walked to one . . .": ibid.
"There is something strange . . .": ibid., 287–288.
"Thies and I realized . . .": ibid., 288.
Danish police officers arrested: Hong, *Occupied*, 283–285.
"It is difficult to describe . . .": Skov, 288.
"filthy muck": ibid., 289.
"By sticking together . . .": ibid., 290.
"We never before . . .": ibid.
"It's a miracle . . .": ibid.
"Flemming and I . . .": Kieler, 256.
"We went off . . .": ibid., 257.

Chapter Thirty
"This was the worst trip . . .": Kieler, 259.
"One side of the hall . . .": ibid., 262.
"We were completely exhausted . . .": ibid., 264.
"But time dragged on . . .": ibid., 268.
"little campaign of hope": ibid., 268–269.
"As our muscles shrank . . .": ibid., 275.
"It was a sharp frost . . .": ibid., 285.
"But the cold soon . . .": ibid.

Chapter Thirty-One
The group sent to Husum also included Viggo Hansen, the
    steelworker and saboteur who had taken part in several
    HD2 operations. He is mentioned in both Kieler's and Skov's
    accounts and survived the war.
"real, ordinary people": Skov, 293.
"Exposure and illness . . .": ibid., 294–295.
"When we returned . . .": ibid., 297.
"Throwing caution to the winds . . .": ibid.
"Our eyes met. . . .": ibid.
" 'Hitler, you failed . . .' ": ibid.
"The rain was slanting . . .": ibid., 298.
"not all of us . . .": ibid., 301.
"Through the cracks . . .": ibid., 302.
"We went across rivers . . .": ibid., 302–303.
Wansleben: http://ic.galegroup.com/ic/whic/PrimarySources
    DetailsPage/DocumentToolsPortletWindow?jsid=f4b82543b5
    3bbedc943e5266238e977c&action=2&catId=&documentId=

GALE%7CCX2560000077&userGroupName=seat24826&zid=
dd5d19a7cf814d34ffd3877121e1ea77. Web.
"It was bitterly cold . . .": Skov, 307.
"Being able to speak . . .": ibid.
" 'You know, Niels' ": ibid., 312.
" 'I wonder if a parcel . . .' ": ibid.

Chapter Thirty-Two
"The work consisted . . .": Kieler, 289–290.
"We were convinced . . .": ibid., 295.
"We still tried . . .": ibid., 295–296.
"The passing of time . . .": ibid., 296–297.
"*Hic mortui vivunt,*": ibid., 297.

Part Five
"Today I was taken before . . .": Malthe-Bruun, 164–168.
Definition: *Oxford English Dictionary.*

Chapter Thirty-Three
Deaths of camp inmates: Yahil, 295.
"My husband comforted him . . .": Oppenhejm, 76.
"Our existence . . .": ibid., 80.
"Was it hope? . . .": ibid., 80–81.
"And then we saw . . .": ibid., 90–91.
"And yet we were leaving . . .": ibid., 91.
Carl Hammerich: see Yahil, 314.
Count Folke Bernadotte: see Werner, 117.
Felix Kersten: see Werner, 116.
Himmler's agreement: see Werner, 117.
"thirty-five white buses . . .": ibid., 118.
" 'The gate was opened . . .' ": Yahil, 317.
"I could not get over it,": Oppenhejm, 92.
"Where to start . . . ?": ibid., 93.
"I have asked myself . . .": ibid.

Chapter Thirty-Four
"If the elevator cables . . .": Skov, 315.
"We walked four . . .": ibid., 316.
"When the sky . . .": ibid., 317.
"It seemed to take forever . . .": ibid.

Chapter Thirty-Five
"We heard that we . . .": Kieler, 303.
"I noticed increased . . .": ibid.
release of Danish and Norwegian prisoners . . . : ibid., 307.
"By way of . . .": ibid., 307–308.
" 'On April 20 the infirmary . . .' ": ibid. 308.
" 'Among the crowd . . .' ": ibid.
" 'I walked as fast as I could . . .' ": ibid., 308–309.
" 'That was her best birthday...' ": ibid., 309.
"The miracle had occurred,": ibid., 310.

Chapter Thirty-Six
"We needed to get warm . . .": Skov, 317.
precarious freedom: ibid.
" 'Hey, they're coming!' ": Skov, 318.
" 'Well, lookit them.' ": ibid.
"our imaginative military . . .": ibid., 320.

Benjamin: ibid., 330.
"The American rapidly fired . . .": ibid.
"Our hearts singing . . .": ibid., 342.
"I bolted up the stairs . . .": ibid.

Epilogue
"In those times . . .": Rittner and Myers, x.
" 'Come back immediately.' ": Ryan, 339.
" 'We had only been flying . . .' ": ibid.
broom handle: ibid., 342.
"So long as . . .": Oppenhejm, 93.
"much better. . . .": Author interview with Niels Skov, October 16, 2014.
"Swim against the stream . . .": ibid.

People in this Book
Ebba Lund: Atwood, 164.

• PHOTO CREDITS •

Pages 162–163: Corbis
Pages 176–177: The Museum of Danish Resistance 1940–1945
Page 181: Votava/Imagno/Getty Images

Part Three: Action & Arrest
Fall 1943–Summer 1944
Pages 184–185: Keystone/Getty Images
Pages 191, 194, 198–199, 222: The Museum of Danish Resistance
    1940–1945
Page 224: S. Bendtsen/The Museum of Danish Resistance
    1940–1945
Pages 226, 227: The Museum of Danish Resistance 1940–1945
Page 228: Ingvar Olsen/The Museum of Danish Resistance
    1940–1945
Page 230: courtesy of Deborah Hopkinson and Diana Skov

Part Four: Deported & Imprisoned
Fall 1944
Pages 236–237: The Museum of Danish Resistance 1940–1945
Page 241: courtesy of Diana Skov

Part Five: Liberation
Spring 1945
Pages 258–259, 264–265, 266, 272, 274–275: The Museum of
    Danish Resistance 1940–1945
Page 281: courtesy of Diana Skov

Epilogue
Pages 284–285: The Museum of Danish Resistance 1940–1945
Page 286: George Rodger/The LIFE Picture Collection/Getty
    Images
Page 288: Keystone/Getty Images
Pages 300–301: Map by Jim McMahon

Photo research: Els Rijper

• INDEX •

Page numbers in *italics* indicate material in illustrations or photographs.

· ACKNOWLEDGMENTS ·

Courage & Defiance would not have come into being without Lisa Sandell, with whom I've had the pleasure of working for more than a decade. An immensely talented writer in her own right, Lisa is a brilliant, compassionate, and dedicated editor. It's not uncommon to shoot off an email at night here in Oregon and receive a response from Lisa right away, though it's after midnight in New York. While Lisa may well be awake at all hours, since she's the mother of two lovely young children, she also manages to extend that same nurturing attention to the books and authors in her care. It is a partnership I treasure.

Lisa is part of a wonderful team at Scholastic, and I wish to thank Phil Falco for his compelling design, photo researcher Els Rijper for uncovering pictures to help bring this period to life, and copy editor Erica Ferguson for impeccable attention to detail. Thanks also to the incomparable Saraciea Fennell, Lori Benton, Ellie Berger, Rachael Hicks, Robin Hoffman, David Levithan, Lizette Serrano, Jennifer Ung, and so many others. I'm grateful also to Steven Malk, my agent, for his counsel and support, and to Michele Kopfs of Provato Marketing for all her help.

It is humbling to attempt to tell the stories of the extraordinary individuals who appear in this book. I wish to acknowledge Diane and Niels Skov for allowing me to visit and for their generosity and hospitality. It was truly a privilege to meet them both. I would also like to acknowledge Dr. Nathaniel Hong, professor at Olympic College and author of two distinguished books on Denmark in World War II, for his perceptive reading of the manuscript. Readers who wish to learn more will find his work illuminating. Any errors of fact or interpretation in the book are my own.

The best part of researching and writing a book like this is the joy of learning. And I learned so much. I relied heavily on memoirs of people who lived at this time, especially Dr. Niels Skov and Dr. Jørgen Kieler, as well as significant work by scholars of the resistance, World War II, and the rescue of the Danish Jews. I am thankful for researchers around the world whose own curiosity and hard work have made learning and writing about this period of time so rewarding. I'm grateful to the parents, teachers, and librarians whose own love of history inspires them to put books like this into the hands of young people.

I am extraordinarily lucky to have wonderful friends and family who support my work. As always, I owe a special debt of gratitude to fellow writer Deborah Wiles for her unfailing encouragement and advice. Thanks also to Janice Fairbrother, Bonnie Johnson, Vicki Hemphill, Elisa Johnston, Ellie Thomas, Deniz Conger, Candace Fleming, Maya Abels, Sara Wright, Sheridan Mosher, Kristin Hill, Bill Carrick, Barbara Noseworthy, Cyndi Howard, Deborah Correa, Eric Sawyer, Teresa Vast and Michael Kieran, Greg and Becky Smith, and many more. Thank you for being there. And, finally, Andy, Rebekah, and Dimitri, I love you so much and couldn't do it without you.

Deborah Hopkinson, December 2014

• ABOUT THE AUTHOR •

Deborah Hopkinson is the author of more than forty-five books for young readers, including picture books, short fiction, and nonfiction. She received a YALSA Award for Excellence in Nonfiction Honor and a Robert F. Sibert Medal Honor for *Titanic: Voices from the Disaster*, which also garnered four starred reviews and was an ALA Notable Book.

Other award-winning works include *Up Before Daybreak: Cotton and People in America*, which won a Carter G. Woodson Honor Award and was also an ALA Notable book. *Shutting Out the Sky: Life in the Tenements of New York 1880–1924* was an NCTE Orbis Pictus Award Honor Book, a Jane Addams Peace Association Honor Book, an IRA Teachers' Choice, and a James Madison Award Honor Book. Deborah is also the author of the forthcoming *DIVE! World War II Stories of Sailors & Submarines in the Pacific* and *Hear My Sorrow*, a Dear America book.

Courage & Defiance: Stories of Spies, Saboteurs, and Survivors in World War II Denmark was a Sydney Taylor Notable Book, a Bank Street Center for Children's Literature Best Children's Books of the Year selection, as well as an NCTE Orbis Pictus Recommended Book.

Deborah lives with her family outside of Portland, Oregon. Visit her on the web at www.deborahhopkinson.com.